ALAN BENNETT

The Habit of Art

D0829166

Alan Bennett has been one of our leading dramatists since the success of *Beyond the Fringe* in the 1960s. His television series *Talking Heads* has become a modern-day classic, as have many of his works for stage, including *Forty Years On*, *The Lady in the Van*, *A Question of Attribution*, *The Madness of George III* (together with the Oscar-nominated screenplay *The Madness of King George*) and an adaptation of Kenneth Grahame's *The Wind in the Willows*. At the National Theatre, London, *The History Boys* won numerous awards, including *Evening Standard* and Critics' Circle awards for Best Play, an Olivier for Best New Play and the South Bank Award. On Broadway, *The History Boys* won five New York Drama Desk Awards, four Outer Critics' Circle Awards, a New York Drama Critics' Award, a New York Drama League Award and six Tonys. His collection of prose, *Untold Stories*, won the PEN/Ackerley Prize for autobiography in 2006. *The Uncommon Reader*, a novel, was published in 2007.

ALSO BY ALAN BENNETT

PLAYS

PLAYS ONE
(*Forty Years On, Getting On, Habeas Corpus, Enjoy*)
PLAYS TWO
(*Kafka's Dick, The Insurance Man, The Old Country,
An Englishman Abroad, A Question of Attribution*)
THE LADY IN THE VAN
OFFICE SUITE
THE MADNESS OF GEORGE III
THE WIND IN THE WILLOWS
THE HISTORY BOYS

TELEVISION PLAYS

ME, I'M AFRAID OF VIRGINIA WOOLF
(*A Day Out; Sunset Across the Bay; A Visit from Miss Prothero;
Me, I'm Afraid of Virginia Woolf; Green Forms; The Old Crowd;
Afternoon Off*)
ROLLING HOME
(*One Fine Day, All Day on the Sands, Our Winnie,
Rolling Home, Marks, Say Something Happened, Intensive Care*)
TALKING HEADS

SCREENPLAYS

A PRIVATE FUNCTION
(*The Old Crowd, A Private Function, Prick Up Your Ears,
102 Boulevard Haussmann, The Madness of King George*)
THE HISTORY BOYS: THE FILM (with Nicholas Hytner)

AUTOBIOGRAPHY

THE LADY IN THE VAN
WRITING HOME
UNTOLD STORIES
A LIFE LIKE OTHER PEOPLE'S

FICTION

THREE STORIES
(*The Laying On of Hands; The Clothes They Stood Up In;
Father! Father! Burning Bright*)
THE UNCOMMON READER

THE HABIT OF ART

The Habit of Art

ALAN BENNETT

FABER AND FABER, INC.

AN AFFILIATE OF FARRAR, STRAUS AND GIROUX

NEW YORK

Faber and Faber, Inc.
An affiliate of Farrar, Straus and Giroux
18 West 18th Street, New York 10011

Grateful acknowledgment is made for permission to reprint the following material: Two extracts from *Profile* by W. H. Auden © 1965 by W. H. Auden, used by permission of Random House. Extract from *September 1, 1939* by W. H. Auden © 1965 by W. H. Auden, used by permission of Random House. Extract from *In Memory of W. B. Yeats* © 1939 by W. H. Auden, used by permission of Random House. Extract from letter by W. H. Auden to Benjamin Britten, 31 January 1942 © 1991 by the Estate of W. H. Auden, used by permission of Curtis Brown Ltd.

The introduction was first published in the *London Review of Books*, vol. 31, no. 21, 5 November 2009.

Library of Congress Cataloging-in-Publication Data
Bennett, Alan, 1934–
    The habit of art / Alan Bennett ; with an introduction by the author.—
1st American ed.
        p. cm.
    ISBN: 978-0-86547-944-9 (pbk. : alk. paper)
        1. Actors—Drama.   2. Theater rehearsals—Drama.   3. Britten,
Benjamin, 1913–1976—Drama.   4. Auden. W. H. (Wystan Hugh),
1907–1973—Drama.   5. Play within a play.   I. Title.

PR6052.E5H33 2010
822'.914—dc22

                                                                        2010014341

www.fsgbooks.com

1   3   5   7   9   10   8   6   4   2

Introduction

By the time Auden came to live in the Brewhouse, a cottage in the grounds of Christ Church, in 1972, I had long since left Oxford, and in any case would never have had the nerve to speak to him. I'd first heard his voice in Exeter College hall sometime in 1955. The lower end of the scholars' table where I was sitting was only a yard or two from High Table where the dons dined, and hearing those harsh, quacking tones without knowing whose they were, I said to my neighbour that it sounded like the voice of the devil. Someone better informed put me right. It was Auden, at that time still with blondish hair and the face yet to go under the harrow.

I don't think I'd read much of his poetry or would have understood it if I had, but when Auden gave his inaugural lecture as Professor of Poetry the following year, I dutifully went along, knowing, though not quite why, that he was some sort of celebrity. At that time I still harboured thoughts of becoming a Writer (and I thought of it in capital letters), so when Auden outlined what he took to be the prerequisites of a literary life, or at any rate a life devoted to poetry, I was properly dismayed. Besides favourite books, essential seemed to be an ideal landscape (Leeds?), a knowledge of metre and scansion, and (this was the clincher) a passion for the Icelandic sagas. If writing meant passing this kind of kit inspection, I'd better forget it. What Auden was saying (and he said it pretty regularly) was, 'All do as I do,' which is what unhelpful writers often say when asked about their profession, though few with such seeming conviction and authority as the newly inaugurated Professor of Poetry.

He used to hold court in the Cadena, but it wasn't a café I cared for. There were undergraduates I knew at whom Auden made passes, though I was still young and innocent enough to find a pass as remarkable as the person making it. When he died in 1973 his death seemed to me less a loss to poetry – the poetry was largely over – than a loss to knowledge. Auden was a library in himself and now all this store – the reading, the categories, the associations – had gone down with that great listing clay-coloured hulk. And though much of what he knew he had written down and published, either as lectures or in reviews, there was always more: the flurry of memoirs and reminiscences of the poet and his talk that began almost immediately on his death, not only a testament to his life but an attempt to salvage some of the wisdom he had discarded in conversation – and some of the unwisdom, too.

In *The Hunting of the Snark*, Lewis Carroll, a Christ Church don, wrote: 'What I tell you three times is true.' With Auden, also at Christ Church, it was the opposite. What Auden said three times you would begin to doubt, and when he'd said it a dozen times nobody cared anyway. Auden somewhere makes the distinction between being boring and being a bore. He was never boring – he was too extraordinary for that – but by the time he came back to live in Oxford he had become a bore. His discourse was persistently pedagogic; he was never not teaching and/or showing off how much he knew, always able to make a long arm and reach for references unavailable to his less well-read hearers. As he got towards the end of his life his conversation and his pedagogy got more and more repetitive, which must have been a particular disappointment to his colleagues at Christ Church, where, when he had been briefly resident in the past, he had been an enlivening member of the common room. Now he was just infuriating.

What they had been hoping for was, understandably, some form of enlightenment and entertainment. This was made plain early on in the *The Habit of Art*, in a speech by the Dean which had to be cut, as favourite bits of my scripts often are:

> The Brewhouse is not a garret, quite – say sheltered accommodation rather. A granny flat. But mark this. If the college is minded to provide this accommodation it's for nothing so vulgar as a poet in residence. This isn't Keele, still less is it East Anglia. No. We see it as providing a niche – young persons nowadays might even call it a pad – for one of our most renowned graduates. If it is a touch spartan, blame the Steward, but then the point of Parnassus was never the upholstery. Besides, the hope is that undergraduates will find their way up the stairs to sit not in the chairs but at these famous feet. But remember, we are not asking the great man to *do*. His doing after all is mostly done. No. We are asking him to *be*. Count the poet's presence here as one of those extra-curricular plums that only Oxford has to offer. Fame in the flesh can be a part of education and in the person of this most celebrated poet the word is made flesh and dwells among us, full of grace and truth.

But to everyone's disappointment – the college, the students, Auden himself – it didn't turn out like that. But say it had been Larkin at the same stage of his life – he wasn't much fun either at the finish.

In 1972, when Auden arrived in Oxford, Britten was well advanced in the writing of *Death in Venice*, his last opera. Neither poet nor composer was in good health, with Auden six years older than Britten. I never met or even saw Britten, but find I wrote about him in my diary in June 2006:

> *16 June.* Having seen the TV programme on which it was based, I've been reading *Britten's Children* by John Bridcut. Glamorous though he must have been and a

superb teacher, I find Britten a difficult man to like.
He had his favourites, children and adults, but both
Britten and Pears were notorious for cutting people
out of their lives (Eric Crozier is mentioned here, and
Charles Mackerras), friends and acquaintances suddenly
turned into living corpses if they overstepped the mark.
A joke would do it, and though Britten seems to have
had plenty of childish jokes with his boy singers, his
sense of humour isn't much in evidence elsewhere.
And it was not merely adults that were cut off. A boy
whose voice suddenly broke could find himself no
longer invited to the Red House or part of the group –
a fate which the boys Bridcut quotes here seem to have
taken philosophically but which would seem potentially
far more damaging to a child's psychology than too
much attention. One thinks, too, of the boys who were
not part of the charmed circle. There were presumably
fat boys and ugly boys or just plain dull boys who
could, nevertheless, sing like angels. What of them?

Britten and Peter Pears came disastrously to *Beyond
the Fringe* some time in 1961. Included in the show
was a parody of Britten written by Dudley Moore, in
which he sang and accompanied himself in 'Little Miss
Muffet' done in a Pears-and-Britten-like way. I'm not
sure that this in itself would have caused offence: it
shouldn't have as, like all successful parodies, there
was a good deal of affection in it and it was funny
in its own right. But Dudley (who may have known
them slightly and certainly had met them) unthinkingly
entitled the piece 'Little Miss Britten'. Now Dudley
was not malicious nor had he any reason to mock their
homosexuality, of which indeed he may have been
unaware (I don't think I knew of it at the time). But
with the offending title printed in the programme, they
were reported to be deeply upset and Dudley went into
outer darkness as probably did the rest of us.

There's a story told in Tony Palmer's superb film about Britten, *A Time There Was*, of how when Kathleen Ferrier was working with the composer on *The Rape of Lucretia* there was quite a serious quarrel (though not with her). Britten tells the story against himself of how Ferrier took him on one side and said: 'Oh Ben. Do try and be nice.' And he says, slightly surprised: 'And it worked.' Both Britten and Auden's works were in better taste than their lives. 'Real artists are not nice people,' Auden wrote. 'All their best feelings go into their work and life has the residue.'

The Habit of Art was not easy to write, though its form is quite simple, because so much information had to be passed over to the audience about Auden and his life and about Britten and his and about their earlier association. Thinking of *Beyond the Fringe*, now nearly half a century ago, makes me realise how I have projected onto Britten particularly some of the feelings I had when I was a young man, not much older than he was and thrust into collaboration (which was also competition) with colleagues every bit as daunting as Auden. Recalling their early collaborations (in another passage from the play since cut), Britten remembers his slightly desperate attempts to keep up with Auden and make a contribution besides the musical one:

In those days I used to bring along a few carefully worked out notions I'd had for the film shots and sequences, but it was no good. Wystan, you see, could never admit that I'd thought of anything first.

'Oh yes,' he'd say, as if I was just reminding him of something he'd thought of earlier. You could never tell Wystan anything, just remind him of it.

Either that or he'd scamper off with your idea and make it his own . . . and not merely an idea. A whole country.

Wystan was the first person to go to Iceland, did you know that? And Christopher Columbus didn't discover America. Wystan did.

While this seems to me a true assessment of Britten's early relationship with Auden, it also chimes with my experiences in 1960. So, though in some ways I find Britten unsympathetic, he, much more than Auden, is the character I identify with.

When I started writing the play I made much use of the biographies of both Auden and Britten written by Humphrey Carpenter, and both are models of their kind. Indeed I was consulting his books so much that eventually Carpenter found his way into the play. His widow, Mari Prichard, was more than helpful over this, though feeling – and I'm sure rightly – that I hadn't done justice to him as a biographer or as a personality. I had had the same problem in *The Madness of George III* when trying to fit in another character who was larger than life, namely Charles James Fox. To have given him his proper due would have meant him taking over the play. And so it is with Humphrey Carpenter, my only excuse being that he would have been the first to understand this and to be unsentimental about it. When he turned up on the stage he tended to hang about and act as commentator, often speaking directly to the audience. This was useful as he could explain points of fact and saved the main characters from telling each other stuff both of them knew already but the audience didn't. Even so, there was still a good deal of explaining left to be done. It's a perennial problem for dramatists and one which Ibsen, for instance, never satisfactorily solved, or, so far as I can see, ever tried to.

Towards the end of the play Carpenter mildly reproves Auden and Britten for being so concerned about their reputations, when their audience, Auden's readers, Britten's hearers, are anxious simply to draw a line under them both. They don't want more poetry; they don't want more music; they want – as they say nowadays – closure. Guilty at occasionally entertaining such thoughts myself apropos Updike's relentless output, for instance, I was reassured to find myself not alone in feeling like this. On the death of Crabbe, Lord Melbourne wrote: 'I am always glad when one of those fellows dies for then I know I have the whole of him on my shelf.' Which is, of course, the cue for biography.

This is the fifth play on which Nicholas Hytner and I have collaborated, not counting two films. Asked, as one inevitably is in Question and Answer sessions, what this collaboration consists in, I can describe it in general terms: discussion on various drafts of the script, for instance, decisions on casting and suchlike, but I can seldom be satisfyingly precise and nor can he. There are no rows or even arguments; neither of us, that I remember, ever sulks. It's so amicable that directors or authors of a more abrasive or histrionic turn of mind might think that the creative process was being shortchanged. However, believers in creative conflict will be reassured to hear that this play has been different.

If Ibsen couldn't explain things it's not surprising that I found it hard, so, whereas Nicholas Hytner had liked the first draft, he was less keen on the second, the script returned neatly annotated with remarks like 'Do we need to know this?', 'Too much information,' and 'Haven't we had this already?'

At this point (though not as a result), in April 2008 I had to go into hospital. This knocked me back a bit and the last thing I wanted to be worrying about was the play. I therefore asked for it to be taken out of the National Theatre schedule (it had been slated for October 2008) until further notice. When I took it up again I found the problems to do with too much information had not gone away, but it occurred to me that the business of conveying the facts could be largely solved if a frame were put round the play by setting it in a rehearsal room. Queries about the text and any objections to it could then be put in the mouths of the actors who (along with the audience) could have their questions answered in the course of the rehearsal.

There was an unexpected bonus to this in that when, as happened on the next couple of drafts, Nicholas Hytner raised objections, these queries, too, could just be passed on to the actors. 'Do we need this?' NH would write in the margin. And on the next draft he would find 'Do we need this?' (his own query) given to the actor. At one point he suggested cutting a pretty tortuous section on Auden's (to me) impenetrable poem *The Sea and the Mirror*. We had a discussion about it and I duly cut it but then introduced the author as a character complaining about the cut. I found all this quite enjoyable, but it happened so often I began to feel the director almost deserved an author's credit.

Less of this, more of that: the director is in the first instance an editor, and so it is with Nicholas Hytner and myself. He likes action more than he does discussion so it's often the more reflective passages that get cut, though they're not always lost. Sometimes they end up in the introduction or, greatly condensed, I manage to smuggle them back into the text – even though this may have to wait until another play comes along: the fractured speech about biography, for instance, that begins the play was actually a casualty from *Kafka's Dick*, written more than twenty years ago. Still, it's a pragmatic process and I'm thankful never to have reached that eminence which would endow every sentence I write with significance and make it untouchable.

There is some talk in the play about Auden's propensity to edit his poems, with his older self censoring what in his younger self he found dishonest or embarrassing. I think he was mistaken, but provided the original survives, which it does both in print and in his readers' heads, it doesn't seem to me to matter much, and just gives editors and bibliophiles something to talk about. To censor one's work is tempting, though. While I was writing *The Habit of Art*, an earlier play of mine, *Enjoy* (1980), was revived. At its first outing it wasn't well received, and were I writing it today there are things I wouldn't include and dialogue I would do differently. That I didn't cut it or alter it I would like to think was from reading about Auden falling into a similar time trap. But if I left the play as it was, it was just through laziness and a feeling that by this time the director and the cast probably knew more about it than I did.

The stylistic oddities in *The Habit of Art* – rhyming furniture, neighbourly wrinkles, and words and music comparing notes – may just be an attempt to smuggle something not altogether factual past the literalist probation officer who's had me in his charge for longer than I like to think and who I would have hoped might have retired by now. Or it may be that whatever oddities there are come under Edward Said's category of Late Style. Feeling I'd scarcely arrived at a style, I now find I'm near the end of it. I'm not quite sure what Late Style means except that it's some sort of licence, a permit for ageing practitioners to kick their heels up. I don't always need that and I'm often mildly surprised when something I've included in a script almost as a joke gets treated in production as seriously as the rest. 'Gracie Fields?' I jotted in the margin of *The History Boys*, and the next thing I knew they were rehearsing 'Sing as We Go'.

The probation officer or the internal censor one is always trying to outflank chimes in with Britten's plea on behalf of constraint, which, while true to his character, is also not unsympathetic to mine. With Britten censorship was home grown, his personal policeman never off duty. Stage censorship itself was abolished in 1968, the year of my first play, so I've never been seriously incommoded by it. On the other hand, I regretted its abolition insofar as it seemed to me to deplete significantly the armoury of the dramatist. With censorship there was a line between what one could and couldn't say, and the nearer one got to this line the greater the tension: How candid did one dare to be? Would the men kiss or the women fondle? After censorship went, the dramatist had to manufacture tension of his/her own.

An author is sometimes surprised by what he or she has written. A play or a novel may start off as having nothing seemingly to do with his or her earlier work, and then as it progresses, or even long after it is finished, it can be seen to relate to themes or persons written about in previous books or plays. It was only when I was finishing the play that I realised that Stuart, the rent boy, is only the latest of a succession of not always similar characters who have found their way into my plays, beginning with my second play, *Getting On*, where he's related to the young jobbing carpenter, Geoff, who is another young man who feels himself shut out (and sees sex as a way in). He in turn is fellow to the rather pathetic young man, Eric, in *The Old Country*, whose complaint is similar to Stuart's (and to Leonard Bast's in *Howards End*). He's less obviously out of the same box as Coral Browne, who, visiting Guy Burgess in his seedy flat in Moscow in *An Englishman Abroad*, pauses by a bookshelf (oh, those bookshelves!), obviously baffled by most of its contents and even more so by Burgess's questions about Harold Nicolson, Cyril Connolly and London literary life. The wife in *Kafka's Dick* is another unmetropolitan waif, and the sports-mad Rudge in *The History Boys*, rather than the sensitive Posner, is the real outsider.

I ought to be embarrassed by these recurrences and did I feel they had anything to do with me I might be. But these personages slip in through the back door or disguised as somebody else altogether and it's only when, like Stuart, they want their say and make a plea for recognition and acknowledgement that I realise the uninvited guest is here again.

I ought to know who this figure is, but I'm not sure that I do. Is he myself as a young man at Oxford baffled by the academic world? Is he one of the young actors in my first play, *Forty Years On*, many of whom I feared would have wasted lives? Is he even one of the procession of young actors who have auditioned over the years to play such parts and who have had to be sent away disappointed?

Some of the yearning felt in this play by Stuart in the houses of his clientele reflects my own wonder as an undergraduate going to tutorials in the vast Victorian houses of North Oxford. I was there on a different, and more legitimate, errand from Stuart, but to see a wall covered in books was an education in itself, though visual and aesthetic as much as intellectual. Books do furnish a room and some of these rooms had little else, but there in a corner the don under a lamp. Sometimes, though, there would be paintings, and occasionally more pictures than I'd ever seen on one wall, together with vases, urns, pottery and other relics – real nests of a scholarly life. And there were wonders, too: drinking soup, once, from fifteenth-century Apostle spoons, medieval embroideries thrown over chair backs, a plaque in the hall that might be by Della Robbia.

These days I think of such houses when I go to museums like the Ashmolean or the Fitzwilliam, where the great masterpieces are plumped out with the fruits of bequests from umpteen academic households: paintings (particularly in the Fitzwilliam), antiquities, treasures brought back from Egypt and Italy in more franchised days than ours, squirrelled away up Norham Road and Park Town, the components of what Stuart rightly sees as a world from which he will forever be excluded – and from which I felt excluded, too, though with less reason.

Acknowledgements

Early on in the writing process I asked Mari Prichard's permission to include her late husband, Humphrey Carpenter, as a character. She and her family have been both generous and forbearing . . . and forgiving, too. As I've explained in the introduction, Carpenter deserves a play to himself, but without his biographies of Auden and Britten mine could not have been written.

I should also thank Libby Purves for her recollections of Carpenter, David Vaisey for his help with Oxford topography, and Patrick Garland and Michael Berkeley for their memories of Auden and Britten respectively, Patrick being one of the few people to have been in the flat that is depicted on the stage.

I am, as always, indebted to Nicholas Hytner for his initial encouragement and help with the text, even if this time we've had more to-ing and fro-ing than usual. Though he carries the whole burden of the National Theatre, he never brings any of its inevitable problems into the rehearsal room. That there are other plays in production or in prospect one might never guess, and I'm sure the actors appreciate this as much as I do. I am grateful to them, too, and particularly to Richard Griffiths, who took on the role of Auden at short notice. One of the blessings of working at the National Theatre is its ample rehearsal schedule; circumstances made ours less ample but they were no less enjoyable for that.

Alan Bennett, November 2009

The Habit of Art was first performed in the Lyttelton auditorium of the National Theatre, London, on 5 November 2009. The cast was as follows:

Fitz (W. H. Auden) Richard Griffiths
Henry (Benjamin Britten) Alex Jennings
Donald (Humphrey Carpenter) Adrian Scarborough
Tim (Stuart) Stephen Wight
Charlie Laurence Belcher/Otto Farrant/Toby Graham
Brian Philip Childs
Author Elliot Levey
Kay Frances de la Tour
ASM John Heffernan
Joan Barbara Kirby
Matt Danny Burns
Ralph Martin Chamberlain
Tom Tom Attwood

Director Nicholas Hytner
Designer Bob Crowley
Lighting Designer Mark Henderson
Music Matthew Scott
Sound Designer Paul Groothuis

Characters

Fitz
(W. H. Auden)

Henry
(Benjamin Britten)

Donald
(Humphrey Carpenter)

Tim
(Stuart)

Charlie
singer

Brian
(originally Boyle)

Author
(Neil)

Kay
Stage Manager

Assistant Stage Manager
(George)

Joan
chaperone

Matt
sound

Ralph
dresser

Tom
rehearsal pianist

THE HABIT OF ART

Part One

*Afternoon. A large rehearsal room in the National
Theatre. Already set up is the interior of the Brewhouse,
Christ Church, Oxford, lodgings into which W. H. Auden
had moved in 1972. There are a couple of easy chairs,
a cluttered kitchen unit and piles of books and papers on
every available surface. The room is a mess.
Above the room and set back from it is another stage
on which is a grand piano. George, the ASM, is checking
props when Donald, who is playing Humphrey Carpenter,
enters, and murmurs to him. The ASM takes Donald's
script in order to prompt him.*

Carpenter (*hesitantly*) I want to hear about the
shortcomings of great men, their fears and their failings.
I've had enough of their vision, how they altered the
landscape. We stand on their shoulders to survey our
lives. So. (*As Donald.*) . . . Yes?

ASM (*prompting*) 'So let's talk about . . .'

Carpenter So let's talk about the vanity. (*He quickens
up.*) This one, the connoisseur of emptiness, is tipped for
the Nobel Prize yet still needs to win at Monopoly. That
playwright's skin is so thin he can feel pain on the other
side of the world . . . so why is he deaf to the suffering
next door? Er . . .

ASM 'Proud of his modesty . . .'

Carpenter Yes. Proud of his modesty, this one gives
frequent, rare interviews in which he aggregates praise
and denudes others of credit. Artists celebrated for their
humanity, they turn out to be scarcely human at all.

3

ASM I thought Stephen had cut all this?

Donald He has . . . which is fine by me, only I just feel, like, the play needs it. You know?

ASM Yeah.

The cast filter in while Kay, the Stage Manager, in her fifties, sets up for the rehearsal of the play, Caliban's Day. *Fitz (who will play Auden) is in his sixties and Henry (who will play Britten) is slightly younger.*

Fitz Am I smoking this afternoon?

ASM Is Fitz smoking this afternoon?

Kay Tomorrow, we decided.

Fitz, who is putting on carpet slippers, pulls a face.

Fitz Worth a try.

Donald My speech about biography . . .

Kay (*waving him away*) I'm doing the setup, love.

Tim (who will play Stuart) comes in wheeling his bike, helmeted and in Lycra etc.
He changes. He's in his twenties.

Tim Afternoon.

Also entering now are Charlie (a child of ten), absorbed in his Nintendo, Joan (his chaperone), Matt (sound operator) and Tom (rehearsal pianist).

Kay (*who has seen it all before*) We're minus Penny.

Fitz Oh. No Penny.

Kay And Brian. Both in the Chekhov matinee.

Fitz Is she? I don't remember her.

ASM Cough and a spit.

Kay I'll read in for Penny. Henry, can you read Boyle?

Henry Will do.

Kay And George.

ASM Yeah!

Kay You do the rest.

ASM Oh, great!

Fitz That's all very well, but no Penny means no cake. You can answer this, Henry.

Tom Coffee, Fitz?

Fitz Why is it that whoever's got the smallest part is the one who brings in the cakes to rehearsal?

Henry Because they're still human beings?

Fitz You see, in my whole life in the theatre I have never brought in a cake. Look at him, they say in the canteen; there is an actor who has never brought in a cake.

He was in *Coriolanus*. No cake.

He was in *Henry VI* Parts One, Two and Three. No cake.

He was in *The Birthday Party*. No cake.

The phone rings on the stage management table.

Kay (*on the phone*) Hello? . . . Leeds!

Fitz The first production I was in here, I was painted bright blue.

Pause.

I was an Ancient Briton.

Kay Oh precious! LEEDS!

Henry I've been painted pink.

Kay (*to various people*) LEEDS!!

ASM Pink! What was that in?

Henry Hospital. I had scabies.

Kay Very good, darling. (*Puts phone down.*) Bad news, people. The director cannot be with us. Even as we speak Stephen is on his way to Leeds, having forgotten he was due to host a conference.

Henry What on?

Kay The relevance of theatre in the provinces.

Fitz Good. So we can go home.

Kay What Stephen suggests we do is run the play . . .

Enter Neil, the Author.

Henry Shit.

Fitz What?

Henry indicates the new arrival.

Oh fuck.

Kay What Stephen suggests we do – hello, darling – is run the play with those of us who are still a little uncertain of the text, Fitz, paying particular attention to the words which I'm sure we would want to do anyway if only out of courtesy to our author, who has just joined us. Good afternoon, Neil. Where've you been, darling? We've missed you.

Author Newcastle, actually.

Fitz Newcastle? Really? What were you doing there? It's all vomit and love bites.

Author I was judging.

Fitz Malefactors?

Author Playwrights, actually.

Pause.

Fitz I am saying nothing.

Kay Now, Fitz, have you your slippers?

Fitz (*displaying them*) I have. I also have my prosthetic cigarettes, my elephantine urine-stained trousers, my disgusting handkerchief and my plastic bag. The question is, have we got the mask?

Author What mask?

Kay gives Author a wide smile and carries on.

ASM The mask is coming.

Fitz They've been saying that for the last week.

Tim (*whispering to the ASM*) Will I be doing the – (*seeing Charlie and whispering*) sucking-off?

ASM Will we be doing the sucking-off?

Author Sucking-off? What scene is that?

Kay silences him with an uplifted hand.

Kay Darling, can we not play it by ear?

Fitz Ear?

Kay indicates Charlie.

Sorry. Though these days they probably know more about it than we do. All right, Charlie?

Charlie nods without looking up from his game.

Kay Right, everybody? Charlie, are you all right? Is Charlie all right?

Joan (*reading*) Charlie's fine.

Author (*to Kay*) Sucking-off?

Fitz If we're starting, I suppose I should have gone to the loo, but it's so far.

Henry Far? There's one just outside.

Fitz No, I can't use that. I don't like to be overheard.
In the whole of this bloody building there is only one loo I can use.

Henry Which one is that?

Fitz I'm not going to tell you. You might start using it.

Kay OK, everybody.

Author Where's Stephen?

Donald (*indicating speech*) Kay?

Kay (*to Donald*) Your speech, love. I know. I haven't forgotten.

Kay's attention to Donald (playing Humphrey Carpenter) should already signal that Donald is high maintenance.

Running Act One. Ready! LIGHTS UP!

Auden and Carpenter are listening to the love duet from Tristan and Isolde *on the record player.*

Carpenter When you were singing that as a child, were you aware that your mother was taking the part of Tristan and you were singing Isolde?

Auden Oh yes.

Carpenter And were you aware of the implications?

Auden I was. I'm not sure she was. My father made no comment. He was a doctor.

8

Carpenter I am talking this evening with Mr W. H. Auden, formerly Professor of Poetry at the University and newly returned to Christ Church.

Auden Am I addressing the nation?

Carpenter Radio Oxford.

Auden Why poets should be interviewed I can't think. A writer is not a man of action. His private life is or should be of no concern to anyone except himself, his family and his friends. The rest is impertinence. Yes?

ASM (*prompting*) 'I was once rung from Hollywood . . .'

Fitz, playing Auden, should keep correcting himself . . . and occasionally be prompted. He is far from word perfect.

Auden I was once rung from Hollywood by Miss Bette Davis. She said, 'Mr Auden, I've just been reading one of your poems.' I said, 'I'm glad to hear it, madam, but it's two o'clock in the morning,' and put the phone down.
    Chester has never forgiven me.

Pause.

Chester is my partner. Is that the word you use?

Carpenter People do.

Auden You can't be arrested for using it?

Carpenter shakes his head.

Not even in England? Progress.

Fitz (*to Author*) People will know, author, this is 1972?

Author If they have any intelligence.

Fitz Because you couldn't be arrested for having a partner in 1972.

9

Author Auden is being ironic. He means it and he doesn't mean it.

Fitz Yes. I know what irony means.

Henry (*on the upper stage*) Actually, you could be arrested for having a partner in 1954, which is why the police interviewed Britten.

Fitz Yes. All right.

Henry And 1972 wasn't such a paradise either. 'How old are you? How old was he?' They don't let up that easily.

Kay On we go.

Henry Someone was had up only last week.

Donald Thank you!

Carpenter (*throws a black look at Henry*) Benjamin Britten is in Oxford today.

> *Auden says nothing.*

Auditioning choirboys. You worked together?

> *Auden still says nothing.*

In the thirties?

Auden I know when it was. Why?

Carpenter I wondered whether there was a programme in it. You and him, collaborating.

Auden That would come under impertinence, I think. My business not yours, though collaborate we did and very happy it was, too.

> *On the upper stage Britten is at the piano with a chapel acoustic. A boy standing beside him sings a verse from 'The Shepherd's Carol' ('O lift your little*

pinkie and touch the evening sky / Love's all over the mountains where the beautiful go to die').

Britten (*over song*) Don't make it sound too polite. 'O lift your little pinkie.' Good. Very good. (*Music ends.*)

Boy Um, sir, what does 'pinkie' mean? Is it rude?

Britten No. I wouldn't ask you to sing it if it were. It's what Americans call the little finger. Happy?

Boy Sir.

Britten Let's try it again and just make the consonants clear.

Fades.

Carpenter That afternoon in 1972 I had gone to interview Auden in Oxford at the Brewhouse in Christ Church, an outbuilding of the college converted into lodgings for one of its most distinguished sons. Spool back half an hour and I am waiting outside with my tape recorder ready to interview the great poet. Only he's not here . . . just a couple cleaning his rooms.

Kay And Henry is reading Boyle and I'm reading May.

Author Why?

Kay Because Penny and Brian are in the Chekhov matinee.

Auden's scout, Mr Boyle, in shirtsleeves and apron, though with collar and tie, is making ritual and ineffectual attempts to tidy the room that is both messy and bleak. Boyle played by Henry, May by Kay.
    Boyle is expressionless, emptying ash from various receptacles into a bucket.

Boyle Jesus Christ!
I was in the Western Desert.

Tobruk.
Ben-fucking-ghazi.
Where were you, Mr Auden?

*May, a middle-aged woman, has come on in outdoor
coat and shopping bag.*
  *Boyle picks up a mouldy soup bowl and shows it to
May. She picks up a cloth.*

May Dishcloth?

Boyle His vest . . .

*Boyle takes the vest, puts it by the sink and retrieves a
pair of trousers that are plainly smelly.*

May Canon Claude's were the same.

Boyle Canon Claude was eighty-five.

May (*referring to soup bowl*) I'll rinse that out.

Boyle I wouldn't. Where do you think he pees?

*She smells the basin as Boyle puts the trousers in the
bedroom.*

May The dirty bugger.

Boyle What I'd like to know is where does he wash his
hands after he has washed his hands.
  Not that he makes a secret of it.
  They were all in Common Room last week after
Founder's Dinner, sitting down to their port and Madeira,
walnuts and whatnot. There's the silver out and the
candles and the wine's going round and the chocolates. At
which point our friend turns to the Waynflete Professor
of Moral Philosophy and asks him if he pees in the basin.
And when he says he doesn't he says, 'I don't believe you.'
This is the Waynflete Professor of Moral Philosophy.
'I don't believe you.' He says, 'Well, I pee in the basin.
Everybody does.' One night – because it's happened

several times – one night it's the Vice Chancellor he's asking where he does his wee-wees.

And he's got another topic in the same department. Toilet paper.

May Toilet paper?

Boyle He's got it into his head that nobody should use more than one piece of toilet paper.

May What for? He must be nicely off. One sheet of toilet paper. What must his underpants be like?

Boyle Mrs Ridsdale. There may not be underpants.

A knock.
Boyle doesn't answer.
Another knock and then the door cautiously opens.

Stuart Hello?

It's a young man, who comes in tentatively smiling.

Mr – (*He looks at a piece of paper.*) Mr Auden? (*Which he pronounces Owden.*)

Boyle Auden. Why?

Stuart I'm supposed to be here at ten past. On the dot.

Boyle So you're early.

Stuart Well, I'm not late. Is it you?

Boyle Do I look like an ex-Professor of Poetry?

Fitz You do, actually. That's just what you do look like.

Kay Fitz.

Stuart So he's not here?

Boyle Apparently not.

Stuart I'll wait then. (*He sits down.*)

Boyle You can't wait here. We're just going.

May Are you an undergraduate?

Stuart No.

Boyle You could be anybody. He has books. Papers. And there's a typewriter somewhere.

May He can't just leave you, not with a typewriter. What are you, then?

Stuart Me? I'm freelance.

Boyle My advice to you would be to go away. Try later. Sit on a seat somewhere.

May There are seats in the Meadows. I often sit there.

Stuart If he comes can you tell him I've been?

May There are more seats in Broad Walk. Then there's the Botanic Gardens. Nice seats there.

Boyle We can't tell him. We're going in a minute.

May Or Corpus. You could sit in Corpus. Some lovely seats in Corpus.

Stuart is baffled, but goes.

He looked a nice enough boy.

Boyle Yes. They often do. I've seen him before. Two or three times. Round Gloucester Green.

May Waiting for a bus?

Boyle Waiting for something.

May At five o'clock in the afternoon?

Boyle What has time got to do with it?

May But Mr Auden's been Professor of Poetry.

Boyle He's been professor of putting his knob in people's gobs for longer than that.

May You're a man of the world, Mr Boyle.

They are going.

Boyle In this college? You have to be.

Carpenter When Auden left his New York apartment for the last time someone in his building was practising 'Show Me the Way to Go Home' on the saxophone. An omen, one might think, but not really; as the Brewhouse is not home and never will be. It's a room that has never made it into literature and one on which its celebrated tenant never wasted any words. Still, poets give voice to the inarticulate universe so it should not seem strange if in the absence of the poet his furniture should take this opportunity to compare notes.

Kay Only Stephen hasn't worked out quite how to do this yet. It's usually Penny and Brian, so bear with us.

Fitz No chance, author, of my coming in on 'it's a room that has never made it into literature'?

Author And cutting the rest, you mean. Why?

Fitz Do we need the talking furniture? I know I'm old-fashioned, but why does the furniture talk?

Author This is a poet. The world talks and everything in it.

Fitz Yes, I can see the idea. And I love the idea. But the bed talking, for instance. It's barmy.

ASM (*brightly*) I know, there could be video!

Which is not well received.

Kay Yes, thank you. Anyway, preciouses, this is what we're doing at the moment. Tom, darling.

Flourish at the piano.
The Furniture is played by Stage Management,
standing in for Penny and Brian.

Mirror
I am a mirror where his squalid reflection
He, shaving, subjects to indifferent inspection.
Morning by morning I see that face,
Dustily return its gaze.
Clint-divided, crumpled, crazed
Like the limestone he elsewhere praised.
The razor's journey like a polar trek
Over crevice and chasm and bleeding neck.
Painfully scraping the soapy blizzard,
That shaking hand on his withered gizzard.

Chair
I'm a chair and in New York
I seated his guests and took in their talk.
I seated Garbo, Pound and behinds both famous and
tender,
T. S. Eliot, Stravinsky and dear Stephen Spender.
Now I'm unsat on as no one calls
To see the odoriferous poet with a face like his balls.
There's the Steward of course, who thinks he's a wino,
Sits on me here and spots cigarette burns on the lino.
Oh call back the days! I just long to be sat on
By bums of discretion, learning and fashion.

Bed
I am the bed that he does not share.
Does anything happen, it happens elsewhere.
A creature of habit, he sleeps on his right,
The one time he doesn't he dies in the night.
But mine are not the sheets of that distinction.
Here is not the place of his extinction.

Auden (*off*) Come up.

Door
He comes, he comes, we've had our lease.
This inanimate colloquy must now cease.

Clock
Not yet, you fools with your fatuous rhyme,
I rule here. I am the time.
Metre, rhythm, scansion, verse.
His life is ruled by verse's curse.

All
Time. Time. Time.

Auden, in slippers and carrying a plastic bag, comes in, leaving the door open. He picks up the telephone.

Auden It's Mr Auden. Should anyone call for me send them straight through. (*He calls out.*) Come up.

He then goes to the washbasin, pees. A young man comes in.

Did we speak on the phone? Stuart?

Carpenter Humphrey.

Fitz Were the slippers round-the-clock?

Author They were. He had corns.

Fitz It's not important.
Do I mime the martinis?

ASM rushes on with props.

ASM Sorry.

Kay (*to Fitz*) I know, I know.

ASM Will you want any of the trimmings?

Fitz Like what?

ASM Cocktail cherry. Umbrellas?

Author (*anguished*) NO.

Fitz The author says no.

ASM I thought that was the purpose of martinis.

Auden I've been to a funeral, though nobody warned me that in Oxford the crematorium is practically in High Wycombe. I thought I'd take a bus, only when I gave him my travel card the conductor said I couldn't use it here. I said, why? He said because this wasn't New York. I don't remember bus conductors being such pedants. I'd only mounted the conveyance out of a mistaken sense of economy. I shan't want the massage.

Carpenter is mystified.

Whoever I spoke to on the phone said there was massage. I don't want it.

Carpenter I don't do it.

Auden What do you do? The funeral service was unspeakable. Barbarous. Whatever happened to 'I am the Resurrection and the Life'? Instead of which there was a lot of twaddle about the deceased having just gone next door.

Auden has been making martinis during this. He now puts two brimming martinis on the table.

(*As he takes one of the martinis.*) Will you want that one?

Carpenter What is it?

Auden Martini.

Carpenter Is it going begging?

Auden By no means. It's what you would call 'spoken for'.

Carpenter By whom?

Auden Guess. How much will I be paying you?

Carpenter Me?

Auden You sound well-educated.

Carpenter I suppose.

Auden And also middle class. As a young man I used to think the lower classes were not fully persons and ought to go to bed when asked.

Carpenter What did they think?

Auden I never enquired.

A clock begins to strike the half-hour.

Auden Here we go. Take off your trousers.

Carpenter What for?

Auden What do you think? Come along, it's half past.

Carpenter What am I being asked to do?

Auden You aren't being asked to do anything. You're being paid. This is a transaction. I am going to suck you off.

Carpenter But I'm with the BBC.

Auden Really? Well, that can't be helped. Ideally I would have preferred someone who was more a son of the soil, but it takes all sorts. In New York one of the rent boys worked at the Pierpont Morgan Library.

Carpenter I am not a rent boy. I was at Keble.

Auden I see. Not a rent boy. Pity. I should have known. The proprietor of the agency – 'pimp' would I suppose be the spade-calling word – described you on the phone as 'chunky'. He sounded Australian. That is often the case with what might be called the ancillary caring services . . . dental hygiene, physiotherapy, the minding of old people, the massaging of middle-aged men . . . These not undistasteful tasks seem to come more naturally to those from Down Under.

Well, at least you haven't brought any of your poetry to read . . . have you?

Carpenter It can wait. Of course. (*Taking out his tape recorder.*) I understand now about the drinks, and the time. As you wrote in *City without Walls*:

'So obsessive a ritualist
a pleasant surprise
makes him cross.

Without a watch
he would never know when
to feel hungry or horny.'

Auden (*cutting him off*) Yes, quite.

Carpenter has taken out a small tape recorder and put it on the table. Auden regards it with distaste.

Carpenter Mr Auden, how do you feel to be back in Oxford? Is it like coming home?

Auden The college has been very kind. I have everything I need, but home? No. Still, I feel safer here than in New York. Just before I left the phone rang and a voice said, 'We are going to castrate you and then kill you.'

Carpenter So what did you do?

Auden I said, 'I think you have the wrong number,' and put the phone down.

Carpenter You've probably been asked this before. Why . . .

Auden . . . did we go to America in 1939?

We went to America because England was too cosy. It was family. And though I like my family I don't want to live with them all the time.

Carpenter But one does want to be with them when they're in trouble.

Auden The thirties were over; now it was war and I didn't want to be the Laureate of Winston Churchill. Besides, nothing I ever wrote in the thirties saved one Jew from extinction or shortened the war by five seconds.
   The truth is, I stayed in America and did not come back when war was declared, not to save my own skin, but because I had fallen in love with Chester Kallman.

Carpenter Why did you not say that at the time?

Auden That I had fallen in love? I would have been put in prison.

Carpenter Are you writing?

Auden Am I dead?
   I work.
   I have the habit of art.

Carpenter Anything in the pipeline?

Auden Hardy would be the model. An old tree, battered, hollow, some of the branches dead . . . (*As Fitz.*) Yes?

ASM (*prompting*) 'But come the spring . . .'

Auden But come the spring still on the farthest twigs putting out leaves. (*As Fitz, to Kay.*) I think I might be reading through much of this.

Kay (*shrugs*) Of course, darling.

Auden Poetry to me is as much a craft as an art and I have always prided myself on being able to turn my hand to anything – a wedding hymn, a requiem, a loyal toast . . . No job too small. I would have been happy to have hung up a shingle in the street:
   'W. H. Auden. Poet.'

Carpenter Which is as good a time as any to say that though Auden does not know it, and nor indeed do I, in ten years or so's time I will write his biography.

Auden The trouble is that nowadays nobody asks me to write anything. I'm asked to pronounce, but that's different. I'm too distinguished.

Carpenter My father said you'd said the same to him.

Auden Your father?

Carpenter You sat next to him at High Table. He's the Bishop of Oxford.

There is a knock at the door.

Auden Ah! My gentleman caller.

He goes to the door.

Bishop of Oxford. Well, of course if I'd taken Holy Orders I'd have been a bishop myself by now.

Stuart comes in.

Stuart I'm Stuart. I came before. I was on time. In fact I was early, only the other guy sent me away.

Auden Quite so. Your appointment, though not your function, has been usurped by Mr . . .

Carpenter Carpenter.

Auden He is not going to be long. You're not from Australia?

Stuart No. Cowley.

Henry A little bag.

Fitz What?

Henry He would have a little bag. The boy. They all had little bags, call boys.

22

Tim What for?

Henry A towel. Baby oil. Stuff like that. Accessories. You could almost pick them out by the bag.

Author I've never read that.

Henry I've never read it either.

Kay So. A little bag. Thank you, Henry.

Henry Thank you.

Kay On we go.

Carpenter Does he keep in touch? Benjamin Britten?

Auden And if he did why should I tell you? I don't know you. You say you're the son of the Bishop of Oxford, but that's no recommendation. I saw a bishop with a moustache the other day.

Carpenter I did actually write to you.

Auden Did I reply?

Carpenter No. I wrote to Mr Britten.

Auden I've never heard him called Mr Britten before. Mr Britten. Makes him sound like a bodybuilder. Did he reply?

Carpenter No.

Auden Take the hint. It's a long time ago.

Carpenter You were both young.

Auden I was never young, not until I was older. Britten was always young. He'll be young now.

Carpenter Whereas you are dead.

Auden Excuse me?

Carpenter As far as Britten is concerned. When he falls

out with someone the ex-friend becomes a corpse. Never spoken of again. Still, he's an artist.

Auden Rubbish. Art is never an excuse for cruelty.

Carpenter So will you talk to me?

Auden I am talking to you.

Carpenter Properly.

Auden No. A lot of what is passed off as biography is idle curiosity, no different from reading someone's private correspondence when they're out of the room . . . and it doesn't make it morally better when someone's out of the room because they're in the grave. If your father's a bishop you ought to know that.

Carpenter (*to the audience*) Writers in particular perceive biography as a threat, something I had still to learn. Poets are particularly vulnerable to biography because readers naturally assume they are sincere, that their verses are dispatches from the heart, the self at its most honest. When the biographer reveals the self is sometimes quite different, the poet is thought a hypocrite. I'm thinking of Robert Frost.

Tim And Philip Larkin.

Fitz Sorry? I'm confused. Is that Stuart?

Tim No. Sorry. Me. I know because we did Larkin for A-level.

Fitz I was going to say. Because Stuart knows nothing, presumably? He's just a rent boy.

Henry Rent boys sometimes find their way to the public library.

ASM Not much trade there.

Author The point is that Larkin and Frost, having supposedly revealed their true selves in poetry, were then shown to be somewhat different. Both were temporarily undone by biography.

Kay Thank you. On.

Donald (*to Kay*) Kay, we still haven't settled where I stand when I'm talking to the audience.

Kay Stand anywhere, dear. Just do it.

Donald And I just go on?

Kay Yes. Be bold.

Donald Standing here? Or there?

Kay There. Wherever . . .

Donald I think here . . .

Kay On.

Carpenter There's another opera, I gather. With Britten. *Death in Venice.*

Auden Aschenbach, the writer in *Death in Venice*, is me, of course. A prisoner of respectability.

Carpenter (*looking round at the flat*) Really?

Auden Respectability is not a matter of soiled clothing or the occasional unwashed cup. I mean that I am no longer employable. I am venerated, monumental, shackled by my reputation. And I need to work or who am I?

Carpenter Which do you think is your best poem?

Auden Another foolish question.
The thing I'm proudest of having written is *The Old Man and the Sea*, an epilogue to Shakespeare's *Tempest*.

ASM I think that's *The Sea and the Mirror*. You said *Old Man and the Sea*. *Old Man and the Sea* is by Hemingway. They had it at the Tricycle once.

Kay (*to Fitz*) Sorry, darling.

Fitz Not that anybody's going to know, anyway.

Kay On!

Carpenter *The Sea and the Mirror* is a poem I can't understand.

Auden It began with me thinking that the end of *The Tempest* really won't do. The injured are made whole, the guilty repent and it's all very neat, but I just felt there was more to be said.

Carpenter What though?

Auden Read the poem.

Carpenter I have.

Auden You should go. I'm thinking of the time.

Carpenter I know.

> 'Without a watch
> he would never know when
> to feel hungry or horny.'

Author Hang on, hang on.

Kay Darling?

Author We seem to have missed something out. What's happened to all the discussion of the poem?

Fitz (*aside*) Shit.

Kay What Stephen felt, darling, was that since Carpenter himself admits he doesn't understand the poem the audience wouldn't either.

Author You mean it's cut?

Kay For the moment, darling.

Author So why wasn't I told?

Kay He was going to tell you, darling, but he had to go to Leeds. You were in Newcastle and now he's in Leeds. We can have a little look at it tomorrow.

Author No we can't. I'm in Cardiff.

If you cut the poem, what happens at the end when Stuart, who is Caliban, comes into his own and addresses the audience?

Kay Oh, we're doing that, darling.

Author What is this play called?

Kay *Caliban's Day*, darling.

Author Exactly, which is prefigured in the poem and you've cut the poem.

Kay We had a little talk about it . . .

Author Oh, a little talk? How did it go, this little talk? One of those 'how do we take the curse off this bit' little talks? One of the 'the author is his own worst enemy' talks? Directing a matter of rescuing the author from the consequences of his folly. Plays, they don't so much go into production as into intensive care. You none of you understand how it works. Yes, it's about Auden, and yes it's about Britten. But it's also about the boy.

Donald And it's also about me.

Author It's like chimpanzees meddling with a watch.

Fitz Charming.

Author Can I reach him in Leeds?

Kay His phone's off. I've tried.

Author Very convenient.

Fitz (*aside*) Kay, I would like to get on. I've got a voice-over at six.

Henry What for?

Fitz Tesco. First of eight, apparently.

Henry Lucky you.

All this aside, but sensed by the unhappy Author.

ASM (*prompting*) 'You should go . . .'

Auden You should go. I'm thinking of the time.

Carpenter (*teasingly*) I know.

'Without a watch
he would never know when
to feel hungry or horny.'

Auden (*interrupting*) Do you mind not doing that? You should not quote a poet's words back at him. It is a betrayal of trust. A poem is a confidence. Besides which many of my poems embarrass me. They don't seem – Dr Leavis's word – authentic.

People tell me off for censoring my poems, rewriting them, or cutting some well-loved lines. I tell them it's because I can no longer endorse those particular sentiments, but it's also because I'm fed up with hearing them quoted. (*Ironically*) 'We must love one another or die.' (*Shudders.*)

In the end art is small beer. The really serious things in life are earning one's living and loving one's neighbour.

He farts.

Fitz That's Auden farting, not me.

Auden What did you say your name was?

Carpenter Carpenter.

Auden Another son of a bishop: Field Marshal Montgomery.

Stuart should have shown earlier signs of impatience, getting up, say, when he thinks Carpenter is leaving.

Stuart Look, mate. I know these university gentlemen. This one's too polite to say, but he shows all the signs of not wanting you here. A more sensitive man would long since have gone for a curry.

Carpenter You don't even know who he is.

Stuart I know this much. He's a client. And I've got a schedule same as you. I'd go.

Carpenter I've gone.

Britten at piano with Boy, who sings "The Ash Grove."

Britten (*over music*) Quite a sprightly start, not too heavy. Lots of words, please, think what they mean. Lovely!

Music ends.

Carpenter Ordering up a youth in those pre-mobile days was not as easy as it is now when the talent can be pictured and indeed sized up on the screen. Then, though, there were no trailers or forthcoming attractions, the thrill of not knowing what you were going to find on your doorstep undiminished by an electronic preview.

But not for Auden. For Auden the thrill was largely over. For him time was what mattered; the best thing about rent boys that they came by appointment. Sex on the dot.

Carpenter should not leave the stage.

Stuart So you don't want the massage?

Auden No.

Stuart And you don't want relief?

Auden No.

Stuart And, have I got this right, you suck my dick? I don't have to suck yours?

Auden That is correct.

Stuart Because it's usually the other way round.

Auden True. But with me the other has always been the preferred option. Weaned too soon, I suspect. Or the tongue speaks the body. (*As Fitz, to Author.*) What does that mean, author?

Author It's a quotation.

Fitz All I need to know.

Stuart How do you want to do it?

Auden How do you usually do it?

Stuart I don't. I'm normally doing the sucking, in which case I kneel. Can you kneel?

Auden It's maybe not a good idea. This is England all over. Hasn't even mastered fellatio.

Stuart Are you sure this is what you want to do? I'd be happy with a straight hand-job.

Auden I wouldn't . . . and I am the client and I'm getting nervous about the time.

Stuart I'm in no rush. Would you like me to take my clothes off?

Auden What on earth for?

Stuart I thought you might like it.

Auden Not particularly, and besides it takes time.

Stuart We're not catching a train.

Auden Get up on the chair. Come *on*.

Stuart For fuck's sake.

He gets up on the chair, lowers his trousers and mimes lowering his pants. The clock strikes six.

Auden Too late.

Stuart Too late for what?

Auden It's six o'clock.

Stuart So what are you going to do? Turn into a pumpkin? Why does it have to be six o'clock?

Auden It doesn't have to be six o'clock. It has to be before six o'clock. It's always been six o'clock. It was six o'clock in New York.

Stuart So? That makes it one o'clock here. Does your dick not know the time difference? I was just beginning to feel like it.

Auden I'll pay. Don't get exercised over that.

Stuart I was just beginning to feel like it. You don't have such a thing as a tissue?

Auden shakes his head.

I somehow didn't think you would.

Author *(puts up hand)* Hello!

Fitz Our author has his hand up.

Author I hadn't thought of it getting so far.

Kay The director would like it to go even further.

Author It's at the end we need to see him.

Kay It will only be his bum, darling.

Tim And I don't mind.

Author The play is not about cocksucking.

Fitz In this instance I tend to agree. And speaking for myself the last thing I want is a nightly vision of Timothy's listless but I'm sure not uncomely genitalia.

Tim I could alter that. The listless part.

Fitz Child. It is too late and you are the wrong gender.

Kay We'll have a little look at it tomorrow. On we go.

Stuart Do you want me to call again?

Auden Provided we do it on time.

Stuart I was on time. I'm building up a bit of a clientele in the university. North Oxford particularly. You get a better class of person than you do in the bus station.

Auden (*paying him*) I can imagine.

Stuart I shouldn't be taking this. I've done nothing. Only I haven't got anything else to offer. I could tidy up.

This plainly would not be welcome.

Auden If you want to earn your money . . . tell me something I don't know.

Stuart Come again.

Auden Everybody has some expertise. What have you learned? What has life taught you?

Stuart Nothing much. I'm young. So far, the only thing I know about – I'm not sure how to put this – the only thing I know about are dicks.

Auden So tell me about that.

Stuart You want me to talk dirty?

Auden No. Certainly not.

Stuart Because I can do that. I go to a vicar in North Oxford. I do that for him.

Auden Anglican, I hope? Church of England?

Stuart Actually I think he's Welsh.

Auden Tell me about your clients.

Stuart I can't do that.

Auden Why?

Stuart I'm a professional. Anyway, what is there to tell?

Auden Are many of them uncircumcised?

Stuart You can't always make out. More uncircumcised in the bus station than in North Oxford.

Auden I was circumcised at the age of seven, which is rather late. Boys who hadn't been circumcised shocked and fascinated me. I was allowed to go to the pictures with the grocer's son. He hadn't been. The genitals are fascinating, too, because they're shape-shifting. Subject to desire obviously, but to fear and cold and . . . Yes?

ASM (*prompting*) 'The innate propensity . . .'

Auden The innate propensity of all flesh to creep.

Stuart Yes.

Auden The penis has a personal character every bit as much as its owner and very often the two are quite different. Have you found that?

Stuart A bit. I've got this old guy. I think he's a professor, small, really ordinary. You'd never suspect what he's got down his trousers. It's amazing.

Auden Men are incongruously . . . Yes?

ASM (*prompting*) 'Men are incongruously equipped . . .'

Auden Men are incongruously equipped . . . Yes?

ASM (*prompting*) '. . . in their very essence . . .'

Auden Men are incongruously equipped in their very essence . . .

Fitz I cannot learn this fucking stuff. I cannot do it.

Awkward pause.

Author Mr Fitzpatrick. Is it me? Do I make you nervous?

Fitz No, but you are in my eyeline.

Author I'm sorry. I will remove myself.

He moves and sits down again.

Fitz Oh, I thought you meant you were going.

Author No fear.

Fitz This stuff about circumcision: this is you, I take it?

Author No. Him. It's in his notebooks. Why?

Fitz I just feel it diminishes him.

Author 'The facts of a life are the truth of a life.'

Fitz It's like the peeing in the basin. We keep focusing on his frailties, putting a frame around them. It's – as he says himself – impudent. It's impertinent.

Author The words are his, not mine.

Fitz There's no nobility to him. No . . . grandeur.

Author He's human. He's old.

Fitz And he talks about dicks. Where – this is what the audience will be thinking – where is the poetry?

Kay Shall we take five?

Donald You see this is where I think my speech about biography that Stephen cut would come in. 'I want to hear about the shortcomings of great men . . .'

Kay Tomorrow.

She talks aside to Fitz.

Is what's bothering you that they won't like you?

Fitz No. Though they won't. I hadn't realised how unsympathetic he is. How . . . coarse. You see, this is why I think he should be reading all the time to give him more . . . credence.

Kay No, darling. The reason why you think he should be reading all the time is so that you can keep a crib in the book.

Fitz No.

Kay You did it in *Hedda Gabler*.

Fitz Did I?

Kay You did it in *Vanya*. If he hadn't been blind you'd have done it in *Oedipus*.

Fitz You don't know what it's like.

Kay I know it's always like this . . . until you learn it.

Fitz He doesn't help, sitting there. 'Mr Fitzpatrick.' They don't realise, playwrights, that you've got to come to it, find a way through. I'll spend a penny. I may be some time.

Kay hugs him. Fitz goes out.

Tim Why doesn't he just . . . well . . . learn it?

Kay It gets harder as you get older. There's more in your head already.

Kay is now with the Author.

He was much better yesterday. You make him nervous.

Author He doesn't know it.

Kay But he's getting there. We haven't had a run before.

Author A run? You call this a *run*? My eighty-year-old grandmother with two plastic hips and crippled with arthritis could do a better run than this. Besides –

Kay Besides what, darling?

Author He just doesn't look like Auden.

Kay Well, I agree he's a bit on the big side, but this is theatre, darling. It's not about appearance. Stephen wants to get away from facile resemblance in favour of the reality beneath. Henry doesn't look like Britten. He's tall, but that's as far as it goes. And Humphrey Carpenter was quite good-looking.

A remark which Donald overhears, though he's not meant to, and is unsurprisingly depressed. Kay now takes it out on the ASM.

You don't ever do what you did.

ASM What did I do?

Kay Correct the actor. Give him the line, yes – *The Sea and the Mirror* or whatever – but don't make him look a fool.

ASM Sorry.

Kay You wouldn't do it to a child, and that's what actors are, children. You keep them happy.

Author Nobody wants to keep me happy.

Kay You don't have to face the audience. You don't have to go over the top like they do. (*Suddenly turning on Tim.*) Are you wearing makeup?

Tim Not so's you'd notice.

Kay But why, darling?

Tim I'm too old.

Kay Darling, you're twenty-five.

Tim I'm twenty-nine. I'm supposed to be a rent boy. I'm not a boy at all.

Kay It's only a phrase. You're a . . . you're a rent person. It's theatre, love, the magic of. Look at Edith Evans. She thought she was young so she was.

Tim She wasn't playing a rent boy.

Fitz comes back.

Kay Now, where had we got to?

Fitz Oh. I'm still on about dicks, surprise, surprise. I just feel he goes on, that's all.

Author He did go on. That was what he was like. He went on. And on. If you can show me a way of him going on without him actually going on I'd be very grateful.

Kay Thank you. Tim!

Stuart I didn't know dicks were the kind of thing you could have a conversation about. I didn't know it was something I had to offer. In a civilised way, I mean, not as a come-on.

Auden Why not? It's human. Nothing more so. I wrote a poem about it once.

Stuart Yeah? Say it.

Auden No. It was bad.

Carpenter (*popping up*) This was 'The Platonic Blow'.

Fitz Oh, for fuck's sake.

Donald What?

Fitz I didn't know you were going to be there, that's all.

37

Donald I've got to be somewhere.

Fitz Do I know he's there?

Author No. He isn't there.

Donald So where am I? Am I in the mind?

Author It's not important.

Donald It is to me. I need to know. Listen. Let's decide this. I feel so *spare*. Can we go back to the start?

Fitz Oh, please God.

Donald I am discovered interviewing Auden after his return to Oxford in 1972. The interview is cut short by the arrival of a rent boy for whom Auden has briefly mistaken me. At which point my part in the story being over, the audience will expect me to leave the stage, but I don't because . . .

Author Because being the author of a literary biography of Auden, and ten years or so after that a biography of Benjamin Britten, you are in a unique position to give a commentary on their lives. You have become . . . the storyteller.

Donald Mr Know-All. I just feel I irritate. I'm in the way.

Fitz That's because you are.

Kay No, darling, no.

Author You irritate him, I agree. But biographers always irritate their subjects.

Donald If this were television I'd just be a voice-over and nobody would even notice.

Pause.

I just feel . . . I just feel I'm . . . *a device.*

Kay A device? Oh no, darling. No.

Donald I am. I am.

Kay You're not a device, darling. I've never thought you were a device.

ASM And even if you are a device it's a very good device, because otherwise they'd all be having to tell each other stuff they know already.

Kay That's right. Device is good.

Henry And anyway, what's a device? Horatio's a device. The Fool is a device.
The Chorus is a . . . well, the Chorus *is* a device.

Kay (*going to Donald*) Oh, darling. You should have said. A device! No.

Kay is holding Donald's hand. It should be Hay Fever *melodramatic.*

Donald Because you see, in life he wasn't a device, Humphrey Carpenter. He was a really interesting, talented guy. I've been reading up about him and all the other things he did besides writing. He had a jazz band. He used to like to dress up and perform. And he practically started Radio 3. Anyway, I just wondered if there's a way of using some of that to muffle the fact that I'm a device – No, darling, I am. And I don't mind being a device if I can somehow use some of the other sides to him to disguise it.

Author (*suspiciously*) Using what? What sort of thing?

Carpenter His music, for instance. Could I just try something out later on, something I've been working on that might help?

Kay I'm sure you can, darling.

And with a look she defies both the Author and Fitz to contradict her.

Something musical, darling. Lovely. I'm sure we'll love it. Going to spend a penny, darling? Love you.

Donald goes off.

Author What fucking music?

Kay raises her hands, disclaiming all responsibility.

Of course he's a fucking device. And what's more, he should be grateful. Actors. Why can't they just say the words? Why does a play always have to be such a performance?

Kay Will you please settle down, Neil! On we go.

ASM (*giving cue*) 'And do you like your job . . . ?'

Auden And do you like your job as a rent boy?

Stuart I hope it won't be my life's work. You get to meet unexpected people . . . like your good self.
  If you don't mind, though, I'd prefer you not to call me a rent boy.

Auden Why not? That's what you are. You are a rent boy. I am a poet. Over the wall lives the Dean of Christ Church. We all have our parts to play.

Stuart I won't always be, though. I do it, but it's not what I am.

Auden No. Though I am condemned to be a poet. (*He gets up.*) I may say that in the unlikely event of your being my neighbour at Christ Church High Table we wouldn't be able to have a conversation like this and for two reasons. Firstly, and obviously, decorum. It would not be thought proper. Secondly and to my mind much more irksomely – because for you at any rate, who are what

I believe some well-meaning persons nowadays call a sex worker – a conversation about dicks is in fact shop . . . and on Christ Church High Table we are not, absurdly in my view, supposed to talk shop.

The phone rings.

Yes? Yes, I see. What time did he say? *What* time? Thank you.

He puts the phone down.

What time is seven-ish?

Stuart Just after seven. Or just before.

Auden Exactly. Not a time at all. Seven-ish!

Stuart Why?

Auden Someone is going to call. An old friend.

He starts ineffectually to tidy up.

You must go.

Stuart nods.

Stuart Can I ask you something? Something personal. Has your face always been like that? The lines and that.

Auden No. When I was a young man – when I was your age, for instance – I was smooth-skinned. I was said once to look like a Swedish deckhand. I still may of course. Who knows what Swedish deckhands look like in the evening of their lives? It's been said that nowadays my face resembles a scrotum.

Stuart N-no. It's what I'd call a lived-in face. You could be quite distinguished.

Auden Thank you.

Britten is finishing his auditions. Donald and Ralph the dresser enter quietly. Ralph carries a box containing the mask.

Britten Thank you. Thank you very much. You still sound rather early morningish, much too late in the day for that. So, why don't we finish off by singing something a bit more jolly and really have a good time?

The Boy sings Britten's arrangement of "Tom, Tom the Piper's Son."

Don't hold back. That's right, it's meant to sound horrid, it's modern music. Smashing!

Auden is now dozing.

Carpenter Film this moment and with the poet alone the camera creeps in to sneak a close-up of the famously fissured face and its congregation of wrinkles.

Kay (*to Author*) I'm not privy to Stephen's thoughts on this one. He's talked about it though.

Ralph (*beckoning Fitz upstage to put on mask*) Fitz, it's here!

ASM brings out a large blown-up photograph of Auden from behind the set.

Author Perhaps he'll get some inspiration in Leeds. If not, when in doubt take it out. It's only a play.

Kay Yes. Well, I think we'll just do it, darling. Tom!

The Wrinkles are played by Stage Management.

Wrinkle One (*played by Kay*) I am one of the creases on the face of the poet. Taken together, my colleagues and I constitute the Touraine-Solente-Golé Syndrome. In a fairy story, solve the riddle of its name and you would be its master, but not alas in medicine, and call it

Touraine-Solente-Golé or what you will, there is no cure and it goes with him to the grave.

Wrinkle Two (*played by ASM*) On the bright side, though, were his face made of the beloved limestone that it resembles our crevices in the cove that is Auden would, like Malham, be host to the hart's-tongue fern, the purple saxifrage and other such botanical rarities. As it is, though, the crud in our cracks goes uncolonised and uncleansed and all we represent is a Q-tip's missed opportunity and a challenge to Botox.

Fitz appears in the Auden mask.

Donald Jesus!

Kay Oh my goodness!

Fitz I'm rather impressed. (*His voice is indistinct.*) What's it look like?

Various Asides 'You look just like him.' 'It's like Marlon Brando.' (*Etc.*)

Fitz You wouldn't know it was me, would you? Hides me completely.

Donald Yes, you're invisible. Save hours in makeup.

Kay Can you talk in it?

Fitz Yes.

Henry Can he remember in it? That's the question.

Charlie, the singer, comes over and stares at Auden, indifferent as ever but at least not looking at his Nintendo. Fitz shakes his masked head to startle the child, which it doesn't, Charlie just giving him another indifferent stare before being taken out of the rehearsal room by his chaperone.

Author Kay, whose idea was this?

Kay rolls her eyes in the direction of Fitz. Author is in despair.

Kay You have to let them try, dear.

Author (*who has his head in his hands*) It looks like what it is, a mask. And if one was wearing a Britten mask and the other a Humphrey Carpenter mask, fine. But . . . it's turning into *Spitting Image*.

Kay We'll see what Stephen says.

Fitz Well, I'm pleased.

Kay You going to wear it now?

Fitz (*taking off mask*) Actually I'll take it off for a minute. It's quite hot, I'll need to practise.

Ralph takes mask from Fitz and puts it in box.

Kay Moving on. Ready?

Auden (*playing and singing at piano*)

Mine eyes have seen the glory of the coming of the
    Lord:
He is trampling out the vintage where the grapes of
    wrath are stored;
He hath loosed the fateful lightning of his terrible swift
    sword;
His truth is marching on.
Glory! Glory! Hallelujah! Glory! Glory! Hallelujah!
Glory! Glory! Hallelujah! His truth is marching on.

Somewhere in the middle of this, Britten slips into the room.

Auden (*without turning round or apparently having seen him*) I was beginning to think you weren't coming.

Britten It's only just seven.

Auden No. It's after seven.

Britten When we haven't seen each other for twenty years five minutes doesn't make much difference. Does it?

Auden (*with an heroic effect*) No. And it *is* nice to see you.

> *They both consider whether they should embrace but it turns into an awkward handshake.*

Britten Should I sit down?

Auden Please.

> *Auden moves something from a chair before Britten sits down.*

Britten I was told you were ill.

Auden I was told *you* were ill. Are you?

Britten Perhaps. Are you?

Auden And so we begin as old friends do, comparing our respective degrees of decrepitude. They say I have a weak heart, whatever that means.

Britten I have a bad heart, too. Sometimes I can't lift my arm to conduct.

Auden Oh, I can do that. (*He does so.*) Though I can't conduct, of course.

Britten Still, I've got a tip-top nurse.

Auden Oh, I haven't. Though there's Chester.

Britten He's not here?

Auden Athens. Peter?

Britten Toronto.

> *Awkward pause.*

Auden Have you seen anybody?

Britten Not especially. Have you?

Auden One or two. Cyril Connolly.

Britten No.

Auden Isaiah Berlin.

Britten No.

Auden Leslie Rowse.

Britten shakes his head.

The Spenders.

Britten Oh yes.

Auden Well, everyone knows the Spenders.

Small pause.

Oh Benjie, I'm sorry. I am so pleased to see you.

He tries to lift Britten's hand to kiss it, but Britten yelps.

Britten My bad arm.

So Auden bends and kisses it and smiles happily. They sit.

I've been auditioning. Looking for a boy. So I thought I'd call.

Auden And did you find one? A boy.

Britten shakes his head.

Britten They were all too perfect. Ideally I want a voice that is just on the edge of breaking.

Auden You want a voice before it gets the mannish crack.

Britten Is that you?

Auden 'Mannish crack'? No, alas, *Cymbeline*, I think. I knew you were here. I saw you this afternoon outside Magdalen. I was getting off the bus. You were getting out of a large car. A very large car. And though it was scarcely raining someone was waiting with an umbrella and there was another person to carry your briefcase. I'm not sure he didn't bow before holding back the indifferent passers-by and ushering you into the lodge. Stravinsky used to be treated like that of course. Do they call you Maestro?

Britten On occasion. Not in Aldeburgh.

Auden Ha! One is struck by the imbalance, the disparity of respect accorded to music over the other arts. Music is a mystery of course, words are not. The deference accorded (which I don't want).

Britten Nor do I.

Auden No, but the space given. The entourage. An upholstered life. Though what I really envy is that you are still working.

Britten's frailty is occasionally noticeable. Auden's a different kind of frailty.

Britten Do you not work?

Auden Every day, but I do nothing. I have the habit of art. I write poems of a cosy domesticity trying to catch the few charred emotions that scuttle across my lunefied landscape. Still, writing is apparently therapeutic. That's what they say these days, isn't it? It is *therapeutic*. When I was young I envied Hardy's hawk-like vision . . . his way of looking at life from a great height. I tried to do that, only now I suppose I have come down to earth. He has taken the words out of my mouth.

Britten Who?

47

Auden Whoever put them there in the first place. But I have to work, or else who am I? What I fear is that on Judgement Day one's punishment will be to hear God reciting by heart the poems I would have written had my life been good.

Britten I have not been alone with you in thirty years, but five minutes and I slide effortlessly back into the same groove, as tongue-tied as ever I was. I tell myself I am not the twenty-three-year-old prodigy mixing the music and doing the sound effects with tin cans in the studios of the GPO Film Unit. I am Benjamin Britten, OM.

Auden OM! I do the occasional reading, mostly in America, where they always love me. The English are more . . . wary.

Pause.

How is Peter?

Britten He's in Toronto.

Auden Chester is in Athens. He's often in Athens. Does Peter have friends?

Britten Friends? Oh, *friends*. Well, if he does I never ask.

Auden You're lucky not to be told. I am. How respectable we have become, both with our long-term partners. What do you call him?

Britten Peter?

Auden Do you say, my friend? My partner? My companion?

Britten I try not to call him anything.

Auden Because neither of us have actually said, have we, both of us just about claspable to society's nervous bosom after a lifetime of our deviant status publicly unaffirmed. I've never felt the need either to pretend or proclaim. So no 'coming out'.

In literature, though, it's different, where a close analysis of my poems and their pronouns has resulted in a tardy retrospective emergence. It is now assumed without it ever having been said. Has nobody in Aldeburgh ever remarked on your setup?

Britten With Peter? No, of course not. Anyway, the ladies of Aldeburgh are iron-clad. Are you out of fashion now?

Auden At twenty I tried to vex my elders. Past sixty, it's the young I hope to shock. I'm unforgiven by the left because I have long since ceased to rally the troops. Still, I *rankle*, which is not unsatisfying.

Britten The last thing of mine that was generally liked was the *War Requiem*.

Auden I missed that.

Britten It was very popular, though that of course turned informed musical opinion off. Stravinsky didn't like it one bit. Now it's Tippett who's way out in front. I'm no longer avant garde. Tippett is the one the students listen to, model themselves on. The money is on Michael.

Auden Art isn't tennis, Ben. You don't have to win.

Britten I'd forgotten that.

Auden What?

Britten When you disapprove, you turn into a school-master and call me Ben, which is what other people call me. You always called me Benjie. He's a nice man, but he's so . . . soppy.

Auden Sorry. Who is this?

Britten Tippett. These days they think I'm arid. Dry. I'm *spare*, I'm not dry.

Auden Does it matter what they think?

Britten I've never wanted to shock. I just want an audience to think that this is music that they've heard before and that it's a kind of coming home – even when they're hearing it for the first time. I want it to seem inevitable. Still, I'm not the darling any more, which should please you.

Auden Me? Why?

Britten You once told me that was what I wanted. To be loved.

Auden Did I?

Britten However we cling on.

Auden That's a misconception. Clinging on.

Britten I'm sure.

Auden We do not contain life. It contains us, holds us sometimes in its jaws. The senile, the demented, life has them in its teeth . . . in the cracks and holes of its teeth, maybe, but still in its teeth. They cannot let go of it until it lets go of them.

Pause.

Britten I have nothing to say. I would add more to your conversation if I just sat at the piano and accompanied it.

Auden When I left New York to come back to England someone in my building was practising 'Show Me the Way to Go Home' on the saxophone.

Britten Yes.

Pause. He plays 'Show Me the Way to Go Home' on the piano.

Auden Benjie. Why have you come to see me now? It can't have been easy. I am a corpse. I was safely dead. Why am I being resurrected?

Britten You're not working on anything at the moment?

Auden Nothing in particular. I work every day. But no. Nobody asks me any more.

Britten I'm working on something. An opera. *Death in Venice.*

Auden Yes, I believe I heard. Good subject.

Britten You think so?

Auden Oh Benjie, yes. Lovely idea. I'm surprised no one has done it before. Made for opera.

Britten It's proving difficult.

Auden Well, it is difficult.

Pause.

Britten Wystan, I was trying to remember, what did we used to do? How did we used to start?

Pause.

Kay And curtain. Tea!

Fitz But no cake. No cake!

ASM Fifteen minutes, everyone!

Interval.

Part Two

The rehearsal room as before, with all the company present except Donald, but including Brian, who is in Russian peasant costume as he's visiting from his Chekhov matinee. Fitz as Auden has the mask on.

Donald enters, dressed in drag and carrying a tuba. He then performs à la Douglas Byng, 'I'm Doris, the Goddess of Wind'. In the course of this the Author enters but says nothing. At the end there is virtual silence from the company.

Donald It was just a thought, only I haven't got the hang of the tuba yet. I wanted to make it plain Carpenter was a man of many parts. (*Going off.*) He wrote children's books. He ran the Cheltenham Festival . . . Oh for fuck's sake!

By which time he's offstage.

Author I am saying nothing.

Kay Leave it with me.

ASM Well, I like it.

Tom Sorry, Kay.

Kay Brian, you should go.

Company say goodbye to Brian.

Stand by, stand by. Ready? LIGHTS UP!

Auden *Death in Venice.* Yes. He was my father-in-law, of course, Thomas Mann. I married his daughter Erika. It was in order to get her out of Germany. What are

53

buggers for? I saw him from time to time. Nice woman, Erika. Not long dead. I was genuinely upset. Still. I am the only one of my family not to get divorced.

He has difficulty remembering this speech, gets cross and roughly takes off the mask.

Fitz I can't do it with this fucking thing on!

Kay (*calling dresser over to Fitz*) Ralph!

Ralph takes mask from Fitz and puts it in box. Donald reenters quietly with stool.

Fitz I'll keep trying, but whatever he says tomorrow, if it doesn't work, I think we should forget it. I'll just have to dye the hair and do the makeup. Besides, it *stinks*.

Kay Makeup can be rather restful, darling.

Fitz It can. It can.

Ralph Baby powder!

Kay (*to Ralph, who is exiting*) Bless you, darling. On!

ASM (*giving cue*) 'So what's the problem?'

Auden So what's the problem? Who is doing the libretto?

Britten Myfanwy. Piper. John's wife.

Auden You mean you're writing it yourself?

Britten No. Though I have one or two ideas, obviously.

Auden There are some writers who set their sights on the Nobel Prize before they even pick up the pen. Elias Canetti is like that. And I'm afraid Thomas Mann. Never underestimate the role of the will in the artistic life. Some writers are all will. Talent you can dispense with, but not will. Will is paramount. Not joy, not delight, but grim application. What were we talking about?

Britten Thomas Mann. *Death in Venice.*

Auden Two of his sisters committed suicide; as did two of his sons. He was a genuine artist.
Chester's in Athens.

Britten Yes.

Auden Where is Peter?

Britten I said. Toronto.

Auden Do you repeat yourself?

Britten is about to answer when Auden goes on.

They tell me I do, but that's not my fault. They treat me like an oracle and that's what oracles do, repeat themselves. Arid?

Britten What?

Auden Your music. I wouldn't have said that it was arid. Detached. Dispassionate. A tune something of an indulgence. But not arid. Do you always *mean* what you write?

Britten In the sense that Shostakovich sometimes doesn't? I think so. Don't you?

Auden I do now. But I didn't always. When I was young I used to leave meaning to chance. If it sounded right I let the meaning take care of itself. It's why I find some of my early stuff so embarrassing.

Britten In those days I'd ask you what a line meant and rather than explain it you'd just write another.

Auden Very naughty. Except that now I'm more scrupulous and make an effort to tell the truth, people say it's dull and my early stuff was better.

Britten Lucky Soviets, I sometimes think . . . composers panicked into popularity. Else martyred into incomprehension. Here, who cares?

Carpenter, who has been on the stage but quite unobtrusively, now moves.

Fitz Are you on still?

Donald Yes. I never really go off.

Fitz But you don't speak?

Donald Not in words, no. I don't speak. But my presence speaks. Which helps, I think. It helps you, doesn't it?

Neither Fitz nor Henry gives any indication that it does.

Look. I am sitting here making occasional notes for their two biographies that I shall in due course be writing, so that in a sense the whole scene is in my head.
I am imagining you.
(*To Author.*) You did mean me to be on?

Author No. But then what do I know? I didn't mean you to sing or get up in drag.

Fitz One doesn't like to think one is just a figment of somebody's imagination.

Donald People. If I'm not going to be a device, I need a story to tell, and writing the books is my story.

Fitz (*mouthing to Kay*) Voice-over. Six o'clock.

Kay Two words: Stephen; tomorrow. On . . .

Donald takes stool upstage and sits in armchair.

ASM 'Myfanwy is very easy to work with.'

Britten Myfanwy is very easy to work with.

Auden Who?

Britten My librettist. Very quick.

Auden We were quick. We were good and by God we were quick.

Britten You were a wizard. No librettist I've worked with since has ever been half as good. I was quite good, too. (*And, since Auden isn't going to say it:*) Yes, you were, Ben.

Auden The boss on the GPO films, Grierson, is revered now, you know. 'The Father of the Documentary.' He was such an innocent. (*Portentous voice.*) 'Ever on the alert, this worker lubricates his tool with soap.'

Britten There are bits of *Night Mail* in the opera, though no one else will spot them.

Auden So do you repeat yourself? What opera?

Britten *Death in Venice.*

Auden He was my father-in-law, you know.

Britten People who've got wind of it aren't keen. They say it's the same old story. Innocence corrupted. Peter doesn't like it. Thinks it's wicked. He says it's killing me.
   You ask me why I came . . . I came because I feel so lonely.

Auden Of course it's lonely. It's new. What do you expect?

Britten I don't know who else to ask. Usually, you see, there's encouragement. Excitement. Everyone pulling together. Aldeburgh, it's a family. This time . . . I get the feeling they're slightly embarrassed.

Auden They'll come round.

Britten No they won't. It's the boy. The man and the boy.

Auden Nothing new there. Of course it's *The Blue Angel*, isn't it, *Death in Venice* . . . with Aschenbach as Emil Jannings and the boy Marlene Dietrich. All for love. I met her once, Dietrich. She wasn't stupid.

Britten The boy is fourteen.

Auden Oh. I thought he was eleven. In life he was eleven. You're not asking me to write it?

Britten Myfanwy's writing it . . . has written it, actually. No, I just came . . .

Auden Because I would be delighted. Nothing would please me more. Myfanwy who?

Britten John Piper's wife.

Auden You say you're lonely. Doesn't she hold your hand?

Britten I'm not sure she cares for it all that much either. I don't know anybody else, anybody else who doesn't defer.

> *Pause.*

It's not so much even that I want help. I just want . . . company.

Auden There's nothing I'd like to do more. I haven't anything on at the moment. There's the odd lecture, but these days they all come out of stock. This would be something new. Goody goody.

Kay (*to the Author*) Okay! (*stopping Fitz*) We think we might know this next bit.

Author Well, someone has to.

Kay (*giving script pages to Henry*) Thank you, Henry. It's Penny and Brian, but Penny and Brian . . .

Author Are in the Chekhov. I know.

Kay Tom.

> *Tom plays. Words and Music are played by Stage Management.*

Words (*played by Kay*) The words of Auden. (*She bows.*)

Music (*played by ASM*) The notes of Ben. (*He bows.*)

Words Once we worked together and now again.

Music But it must work, this revived hook-up.

Words Or *Death in Venice* will be a fuck-up. (*Words takes back script pages.*)
   I'm nervous.

Music Don't be. They're chums. And Ben is a sweetie.

Words Wystan, too . . . in his way.

Music The gang, that's the operas, the chamber music, the *musica totalis* . . . we adore Ben. He's our creator, after all.

Words He's never . . . ashamed of you?

Music Ashamed? Of his compositions? Why should he be? We're his children. Wystan's not ashamed of you?

Words No . . . but he is a perfectionist.

Music So is Ben. And he loves to show us off and we get to no end of places. The Wigmore Hall, the Purcell Room, the BBC Studios in Maida Vale. Then when it's all over its back to Snape to compare notes. Do you go abroad at all?

Words Austria in the Summer. New York.

Music New York? Pff. We're just back from Valparaiso!

Words You like Ben. But does Ben like you?

Music Like us? No! He loves us!

Words It's never, 'Do I mean that still?'

Music No.

Words Never, 'Was I being sincere?'

Music The idea.

Words Look.
I have to come clean. We, the poems, the stuff he's written . . . we are sometimes hated.

Music Hated? But he wrote you.

Words We embarrass him. We embarrass him so much several of my colleagues never even made it into the *Collected Poems*.

Music No!

Words Excluded. Purged.

Music Purged?

Words Never spoken of again. There was *Spain*, a perfectly good poem cut out completely. Another one, *September 1, 1939*, he had 'second thoughts' about. And you can't do that, you see. It makes the rest of the oeuvre very nervous . . . I mean, who's going to be next?

ASM shakes head sadly.

Music Dear me. I don't like the sound of this.
Still let's look on the bright side: people only listen to the music; nobody listens to the words.

Words That's what Wystan says. (*As Kay.*) Moving on.

Auden What's it like, Myfanwy's libretto?

Britten Very good. Just the ticket. I'm not sure she always understands the book quite, but it's good. It's good.

Auden Does she surprise you?

Britten She is a bit naive.

Auden No, no. Does she show the subject in an unexpected light? Does she surprise you into music?

Britten Well . . .

Auden In the opera house words themselves go for nothing. An operatic audience doesn't listen to the words and only hears maybe one in five. But that's not the point. The librettist's function comes earlier because what the librettist, the writer of the words, has paradoxically to do is deliver the music. The librettist is a midwife . . . But it's a while since I read *Death in Venice*. Remind me.

Britten Aschenbach is a famous author respected –

Auden That's right, and more to the point, respectable –

Britten Married with a daughter, his wife is dead –

Auden That's right –

Britten – and he takes himself off to Venice where he stays on the Lido. He's suffering from writer's block.

Auden Oh, I'd forgotten that. It's not a complaint from which I've ever suffered . . . or entirely believe in. Whatever form it takes there is never any fun reading about constipation. It assumes, too, that the natural condition of writers is writing whereas the natural condition of most writers is not writing.
  Have you ever had composer's block?

Britten No, though people do. Walton, for instance, takes his time. Anyway, Aschenbach is in the hotel –

Auden Yes, where he sees – I don't recall him ever speaking to – a Polish family with a beautiful son of fourteen, with whom he becomes obsessed. Tadzio.

Britten Aschenbach gazes at the boy, besotted with his beauty and thinking in this way to recharge his batteries.

Auden Yes, that's it. He's supposed to be looking for inspiration. But if he wants to look at a beautiful boy, why does he need an excuse? You never do.

Britten There's an epidemic of cholera in mainland Venice –

Auden That's right, which the authorities are anxious to hush up, though the whole city reeks of carbolic. He ought to leave but fascination with the boy keeps him on the Lido and in the process makes him dye his hair, paint his face and lose all dignity. Eventually he contracts cholera and dies on the beach, still gazing adoringly at Tadzio, whose final gesture seems to beckon him out to sea, with the implication being that he, Tadzio, is also an angel of death.

Britten You remember it very well.

Auden Well, he was my father-in-law. Isn't Myfanwy Piper one of those big girls that Betjeman likes? Or pretends to. He always used to say it was boys with him but that was John just wanting to be in the swim. How is Betjeman?

Britten shakes his head.

In Oxford the other day apparently. He's supposed to like Oxford. Never comes to see me.

Britten (*who has a copy*) I've known the novel all my life.

Auden Of course. We all have. It's a queer set book.

Britten And Thomas Mann is Aschenbach, presumably.

Auden Their predicament is the same. The eye for male beauty. The occluded sexuality. God, he could be pompous.

He has taken the book from Britten.

'He thought of his fame, reflected that many people recognised him in the street and would gaze at him respectfully, saluting the unerring and graceful power of his language.'

Pompous ass.

Still, it's a good story with all the unfulfilled longing in the music. Think what Strauss could have done with it.

Britten smiles heroically in the circumstances.

Britten Tact was never your strong point.

Auden Lots of lagoon stuff of course. The sea. The sea is your thing, isn't it?

Britten So I'm told.

Auden That's right. Extravagant, unacceptable, and the love literally unspeakable but not unsingable, it's made for opera. And made for you. 'Whereof we cannot speak, thereof one sings.'

Britten It scares me.

Auden That's good, Benjie.

Britten It comes quite close to home.

Auden So it should.

Britten It touches on stuff I can't really talk to Myfanwy about. Though she's a nice woman. To do with me, obviously. Though she probably knows.

Auden I'm sure she does.

Britten I don't mean she's a prude. The reverse, really. The boys' beach games, for instance. She wants Tadzio and his friends to dance naked. I think there might be problems about that.

Auden The closer you can steer to yourself the better it will be.

Britten This is Tadzio's music.

He plays it on the piano.

As I say, people don't like it already.

Auden The music? We-e-ll . . .

Britten No, not the music. The story. They are uneasy about the story.

Auden What people?

Britten In Aldeburgh. I've only mentioned it to a select few, but word gets round. 'Here we go again,' is what they're saying. '*Peter Grimes*, *Billy Budd*, *The Turn of the Screw*. Britten's perennial theme of innocence corrupted.' Sometimes I think they'll come for me as they came for Grimes.

Auden Why should they? They know the score. Half of them have thrown their boys at you in the first place. But they're not keen?

Britten Not so far.

Auden I am.

Britten Wystan.

Auden I am. I long to do it.

Britten Wystan. All I want is help.

Auden But I can write the whole thing. Won't that be a help?

Britten But it's promised for next year's festival.

Auden So? We've done it before. We used to polish off a film in a week. And it's so long since I had anything worthwhile to do, it will be sheer pleasure.

Britten What about Myfanwy?

Auden Ditch her. You're queer. They expect you to break your promises. I wish Chester were here. He'd love it.

Auden gets hold of the script and starts going through it.

64

Britten No. All I need is somebody – you – to tell me I've got it right.

Auden Who will sing Aschenbach?

Britten Peter, of course.

Auden Peter?

Britten *Peter.*

Auden Peter. Oh of course. Don't need that. (*He puts a line through a page of the libretto.*)

Britten Some people – some critics – don't care for his style of singing, but they've come round to it. It's true his voice has its limits but he has made them see that it is beautiful.

Auden That is the nature of style. It imposes itself. Do without that. (*Another crossing out.*) . . . Style is the sum of one's imperfections . . . what one can't do, as much as what one can . . .

Auden is still going through the libretto, ticking and crossing.

It's all right, this. It will do, I'm sure. But we can do better. Tell me about the boy. How old should he be?

Britten Myfanwy and I thought we might get away with seventeen.

Auden You mean with the audience?

Britten Yes.

Auden Because in the book he's fourteen.

Britten Well, sixteen then. It depends what he looks like.

Auden Or whatever age it is nowadays that beauty can be legally admired. The boy Thomas Mann actually saw and took a fancy to was eleven. He wrote him up as being fourteen. Now you're suggesting sixteen. At this rate he'll soon be drawing a pension.

Britten Wystan, you have to take the audience with you.

Auden Ben, why are you still sending messages in code? These days you can come clean.

Britten About fourteen-year-old boys? I don't think so.

Auden In the music you can.

Britten This isn't the music. This is the libretto.

Auden And the libretto shapes the music, as I've explained. Doesn't Aschenbach have a dream in which he is shocked to find he lusts after the boy? (*Looking at the script again.*)

Britten He does, yes. He sees him as a vision of Apollo.

Auden (*crossing out again*) Well, we can lose that for a start. This is a novelist. A self-proclaimed man of the world. He doesn't need a dream to tell him he fancies someone.

Britten It puts it into context.

Auden And coming from the subconscious makes it respectable. Apollo, Dionysus. Tosh . . . it's a boy on a beach.

Britten You don't understand. In the book Aschenbach is the innocent. He is seduced by beauty.

Auden That's why you were attracted to it? Presumably because at sixty-eight, or whatever he is, Aschenbach is the innocent and the boy leads him on? You fancy it the story of your life.

Britten No. No. Stop! Stop! (*He covers his ears.*) It's too soon. You haven't changed. You ask too many questions, just like you always did. I don't know the answers yet and I only find the answers through the music. Ask too many questions too soon, and I never will because it won't get written. I have to write it before I can write it, can't you see that? In the book –

Auden Ben, fuck the book. I can't write a furtive libretto. You like boys, Ben. No amount of dressing Tadzio up as a vision of Apollo can alter the fact that Dionysus for you comes in a grey flannel suit or cricket whites. This is an old man lusting after a boy, and Apollo has got fuck all to do with it.

Britten Wystan. How many more times? Aschenbach is the innocent. In the story it is the boy who is the tempter. If all my operas are concerned with the loss of innocence, well, in this one the innocence is – the old man's.

Auden What does it matter? Why does innocence come into it? Neither of them are innocent. It's not corruption. It's collaboration.

Long pause.

Britten Constraint, that's what you've never appreciated.

Auden Rubbish. A poet is governed by constraint, by metre and form.

Britten No, I mean where subjects are concerned. Where this subject is concerned. You don't believe in restraint. I do. I always have. And I hope I never see the day when in opera or in drama there is nothing that cannot be sung or said. A time of no limits.

Auden This is England talking, isn't it, Ben? This is taste, modesty, self-restraint. The family virtues. Except that you don't belong in a family any more than I do. And you're harder to spot. Lovable, sought after, beautifully mannered; the parents didn't mind, maybe, but you were the predator.

Britten No. No. (*To Author. As Henry.*) Is it true about the parents? Didn't they mind?

Author The fathers could be uneasy. The mothers didn't seem to mind at all.

Fitz Dear Ben.

Henry Did anything happen?

Author (*shrugs*) There were boys all through his life to whom he gave his heart. Sometimes he was loved in return. And licensed.

Henry And that's when Aldeburgh looked the other way.

Author He seems to have been drawn to boys who knew the score. Who didn't flinch at the occasional hug or were unabashed when the naked composer came and sat on the side of the bath. 'What a funny boy you are.'

Henry But no one ever complained?

Author So far as we know, the worst Britten inflicted on these beloved youths was occasional embarrassment.

Kay Mmm. On . . .

Britten If I like boys . . .

Auden Ben, there is no 'if' . . .

Britten All right, all right. Listen. For once in your life, *listen*. I don't prey on them. They like me if only because I . . . attend to them. I listen. And since many of them are musical we play together . . . musically. Even the ones I cannot touch I can play with. And maybe one sort of playing is a substitute for another sort of playing, but it means we can do things together and perfectly properly. There is no threat in a duet. Or . . . playing the teacups.

Auden Still, it's a dangerous game. Imagine the scene – you have, I'm sure. A middle-aged man wakes up one morning, unemployed mostly but who gets by giving violin lessons or doing music copying . . . some ex-Tadzio who decides those high times in Aldeburgh were when his life took the wrong turning. So being a dutiful citizen he goes down to the police station, though not of course in Aldeburgh, and tells his story. Then you wake up.

The model pupils of this world believe that artists have to pay, otherwise it isn't fair. You've never really paid, have you?

Britten Not paid? I'm dying.

Auden Ben, Ben. Death isn't the payment. Death is just the checkout. (*Pause.*) I've failed the test, haven't I?

Britten There was no test. I needed a hand. Not with the writing. Someone to say, 'Go on. Go on.' You used to be good at that. But you were always a bully. I'm too old for that.

Auden And too celebrated. Too loved. But so you've always been. Still, it's nice you thought of me. People don't, nowadays, much. So. What do I say to you, Benjie? I say, 'Take no notice. Go on, my dear.'

Britten Even with Myfanwy?

Auden Even with Myfanwy and Apollo and Dionysus and all that counterfeit classical luggage. We know it's boys, Benjie.
 Let everybody like you.
 Let them love you.
 But go on. Go on.

Britten 'Wherever you go and whatever you do you will always be surrounded by people who adore you, nurse you, praise everything you do, and you build yourself a warm little nest of love by playing the lovable talented little boy.'

Auden Who said that? It's very good.

Britten You did. It's a letter you wrote me when we parted in New York in 1942. And you said if I was ever to grow up I would have to learn how to be a shit.

Auden Well, you've managed that. Oh, not with me, but with all the other friends you've turned your back on. Still, dear Benjie, I'm glad you came. And – Myfanwy permitting, of course – I could still help out with the libretto. I knew him, you see. Mann was my father-in-law. Did I tell you that?

Britten When I was a boy – because at twenty-three I was still a boy – I was baffled by the torrent of words that used to pour out of you and I clung to my pathetic staves and bar lines lest I drown in your wake. These magnificent words – I used to think my paltry music just an afterthought, a servant to the words. But it's not. Music melts words . . . your words and Myfanwy's, too. It's the music that matters, even in Gilbert and Sullivan. Music wins.

Carpenter And to Britten winning was important.

He rises from his chair and re-enters the action.

Silenced earlier, now I should speak, since as biographer to you both I am your passport to posterity.

Auden The cheek. Our passport is what we have written.

Britten Quite. Those who love and admire us. I am sure of that.

Carpenter Are you? Would it not surprise you to learn that there is a growing number of your devotees who would in the nicest possible way be happy to see you dead?

Britten Dead? Me?

Auden Not in Milwaukee. They loved me in Milwaukee.

Carpenter Not another opera, not more poems: a funeral.

Britten I've still got so much to do.

Auden I want to write this libretto.

Carpenter There's no malice in it. It's just an entirely human desire for completion . . . the mild satisfaction of drawing a line under you. Death shapes a life.

Dead, you see, you belong to your admirers in your entirety. They own you. They can even quote you to your face – only it will be a dead face – at your memorial service perhaps, or when they unveil the stone in Westminster Abbey. Over and done with: W. H. Auden. Benjamin Britten. Next.

Fitz Not the same with actors, though, is it?

Author Why?

Fitz They're not waiting for us to go?

Author Yes, but actors aren't always breaking new ground the way writers or composers are supposed to do. Actors can just be more of the same.

Fitz With me?

Kay Yes, with you, darling, and it is more of the same with actors most of the time. As you'd know if you were in the corner every night. They all have their little canteens of histrionic cutlery – Larry's sudden fortissimos, John G.'s tremolo . . .

Fitz It's known as style.

Kay I was in the corner for something Alec did.

Tim Alec who?

Kay On one particular line he used to do a little flick of his leg. Cut to five years later when I worked with him again . . . different play, same flick. Fool that I was, I made the mistake of mentioning it to the director, and fool that he was, he made the mistake of mentioning it to Alec. Result was he didn't speak for four days. But they all do it. Great acting is a toolbox.

Fitz Lucky not to get the sack.

Kay Which we will if we don't get on.
(*Giving cue.*) 'Why do you do this?'

Britten Why do you do this? Write biography? Why not make your own way in the world instead of hitching a lift on the life of someone else?

Auden I would find it intolerable myself if only because of the degree of self-relegation involved. A biographer is invariably second-rank even when he or she is first-rate.

Britten That said, whose life will make the better read? Wystan's, I imagine. Berlin. New York. Ischia. What have I got? Aldeburgh.

Carpenter And the boys.

Britten gets up, ready to go.

Britten I must go.

Auden (or Fitz) has fallen asleep.

Henry The question is, is he asleep as Fitz or is he asleep as Auden?

Author Auden could go to sleep here, actually. It's quite plausible.

Kay Don't suggest it. It would be the thin end of a very long wedge.

Fitz I'm not asleep.

Kay Yes, you were, darling.

Fitz I'm smoking tomorrow, that will help.

Britten I must go.

Auden Will you call me? They put calls through from the Lodge. I could start any time.

Britten I'll talk to Peter.

Auden Give him my love. Tell him how I've changed.

Britten We've both changed.

Someone comes running up the stairs. It's Stuart.

Stuart Oh, sorry.

Auden This is a friend of mine . . . What was your name again?

Stuart Stuart.

Auden This is Mr Britten.

Pause.

Stuart Why I came back . . . I'm not interrupting anything?

Auden Is he? Is he interrupting anything, Benjie?

Britten No. We're . . . we're finished.

Stuart Why I came back was that the old guy I go to in Norham Road. I told him where I'd been – which I wouldn't normally do because I don't talk about clients – and he said I should come back, that you were famous and it would be something to tell my grandchildren about.

Auden That depends on whether you're going to have any grandchildren.

Stuart Oh yes. This is just a phase.

73

Auden And on how enlightened these putative grandchildren turn out to be. 'Your grandpa was once a rent boy' is hardly a bedtime story.

Stuart I told you. That's not a job description I answer to. Only, the thing I don't understand is this . . . The guy I go and see, he'll open the door and there are books everywhere, books in the hall, books on the landing, books and pictures . . . proper pictures, not prints. And he's sitting there under the lamp in front of the fire and the clock's ticking and the sherry's poured. And he's playing classical music on what he calls his radiogram . . . It's just lovely.

Auden In which case, you should go and see Mr Britten.

Stuart Only then he tells me to come back here because you're the great man . . . and look at it. Look at you. It's a shit heap. Of course, however cosy it all is, he still wants me to take it out. Only I feel that pollutes it. I thought it was either/or. I never thought guys like him even did it. He doesn't look as if he does. I thought he was respectable.

Auden Then you're very old-fashioned.

Stuart You asked me, earlier on, what did I know? One thing I've learned is that given the chance everybody does it, one way or another. It's not much of a lesson, though, is it?

Fitz You don't feel, author, that you're glamorising this young man? Sorry, Tim. Would someone as sensitive – as potentially refined even – as you're making him out to be, would he go on the game?

Author It's possible.

Tim I can understand why he doesn't want to be called a rent boy.

Fitz Oh yes, dear boy. But would he *be* a rent boy?

Kay That's not really for you to ask, is it?

Fitz I have to play the scene.

Tim Am I doing it wrong?

Kay No. Absolutely not. Fitz. (*And she shakes her head in disapproval.*)

Henry When I was at RADA in the seventies someone I knew – a friend – was very hard up. And he went on the game.

Donald Poor sod.

Tim Why? It might be quite enjoyable. That was pretty well pre-everything then, wasn't it? No risk and that.

Kay How did it work? Did he hang around in Piccadilly?

Henry No, no. It was classier than that. It's like everything else in life. You get yourself an agent. The clients rang the agency, the agency rang him and he went round like he does in the play.

Kay What were the others . . . the other boys? Were they full-time?

Henry All sorts, one was a waiter, another worked at the Air Ministry. One was a porter at Sotheby's.

Tim What did your friend say they were like, the clients? Did he feel badly about it?

Henry Who?

Tim Your friend.

Henry No, he didn't feel badly about it at all. Only one evening he went round to a new client . . . and it was one of the teachers from RADA.

Fitz Did they do it?

75

Henry The teacher offered to help him with his fees, so he more or less stopped doing it after that.

Fitz More or less? Did he still have to sleep with the teacher?

Pause.

Henry Now and again.

Kay Life.

Henry Yes.

Kay Come on. Last lap.

Henry What I was meaning is – it can be quite ordinary most of the time. A job. Not degradation.

ASM (*giving cue*) 'I'd better be going.'

Britten I'd better be going.

Auden No, we haven't finished.

Britten Wystan, we have.

Auden Besides, you can tell your grandchildren about this gentleman, too.

Stuart Yeah? Are you somebody, then?

Britten No, I'm just a friend of Mr Auden's.

Auden A friend from way back.

Stuart Everybody knows everybody.

Auden Well, having brought you two together, I think I might spend a tactful penny . . . though I'll pay you both the compliment of doing it in the bathroom.

Auden goes out. Awkward pause.

Stuart Are you more famous or less famous? One to ten.

Britten Both about eight.

Stuart You're more normal. You don't smell, for a start. So should I remember you when I'm old?

Britten Ask your man in Norham Road. You'd be better playing the music. And with Wystan, reading the poetry.

Stuart So was he sexy?

Britten Looking, you mean? No. But you didn't ever want to be with anyone else.
   And talking always. People went to bed with him to stop him talking . . . though it didn't.
   Young men aped the way he talked, aped how he dressed. And wrote how he wrote, or tried to. He was . . .

Stuart A star.

Britten Yes, I suppose. Are you . . . musical at all?

Stuart No.

   Pause.

Are you?

Britten I am, yes, a little.

Stuart Great. What sort of thing?

Britten Oh, highbrow stuff mainly. Orchestras. Singing. Opera.

Stuart Great. Great.
   (*To the audience.*) This is when I wish I was round the back of the bus station. Then, there's no talk. If I met this guy round Gloucester Green, we wouldn't have to go through all this . . .

   Britten plays a chord.

I've never seen an opera.

Britten That's good. I wrote an opera for boys like you who'd never seen one.

Stuart Yeah?

Britten It was quite jolly. Some of them couldn't play or sing but they did the music with drums and teacups.

Stuart Teacups?

Britten Yes. And the audience sang, too.

Stuart Did you have to pay them?

Britten The audience? No. No. They did it for . . . well, for love, I suppose. I live in Suffolk. People . . . people like me there. Perhaps you could come there one day.

Stuart Suffolk? Yeah. I'd like that.

Carpenter Britten's boys generally had more to offer than this. Their voices, for a start; they could read music; some of them could play music, even compose it. They were accomplished young men. All this boy has to offer is his dick.

Stuart So? Do you think I don't know that?

Britten Do you think I don't?

Auden returns.

Auden Are you going, Benjie? Hold my hand for a second.

Britten having gone out, Auden thinks of something and runs to the top of the stairs.

And remember, Ben. Fuck Aldeburgh. And while you're at it, fuck Glyndebourne! But Ben. *Go on.* Ah, Boyle.

Boyle (read by Henry), who is coming up the stairs with a tray, must have caught the full force of these imprecations, but he is as imperturbable as ever.

78

Boyle Not disturbing you, am I, sir? You missed dinner. That's not like you. The Dean was worried. He thought you might have died.

Auden No such luck. And . . . a sentence I never thought I'd hear myself utter: I forgot the time.

Boyle lays out the dinner.

(*To Stuart.*) Have you had anything to eat?

Boyle Oh, come along, sir.

Auden It's too late for me.

Stuart Are you sure?

Auden Please.

Boyle maybe pours him a glass of wine while looking murderous.

Boyle Professor Tolkien was dining in hall, sir.

Auden That's a shame. I like him.

Boyle Written another book, apparently.

Auden Really? More fucking elves, I suppose.

Boyle That was Mr Britten, wasn't it? Big car. Chauffeur. Probably writes commercials. Jingles. It's how they all make their money nowadays, musicians.

Nothing else you want? I'll say goodnight.

Stuart (*maybe toasting him*) Goodnight.

Boyle doesn't dignify him with a reply.

Auden Late. Nine o'clock.

Stuart You could still suck me off.

Auden As a nightcap, you mean? I prefer Scotch. Were you ever innocent?

79

Stuart What of? I haven't done anything.

Auden Untouched. Unfingermarked.

Stuart When I was young. Still am young, I suppose. Though not untouched, obviously.

Auden Do you blame anybody?

Stuart shrugs.

Stuart (*looking at the room*) Do you?

Auden smiles.

Auden Dirt is everywhere.

Stuart Not on people. Also there's no need to stink. Not these days.

Auden Maybe you should be a nurse.

Stuart I thought of that. Another job where you fiddle with people and take dicks for granted.

Auden has put on a record and now plays the first of the 'Four Sea Interludes' from Peter Grimes.

(*To the audience.*) He asked me all sorts of questions. I asked him nothing. Later, much much later, when all these people were dead, I started to read and it discovered to me what my questions should have been. These unasked questions reproach me still.

Carpenter Both their deaths were appropriately located: Auden, aged sixty-six, a transient's death of a heart attack alone in a middling hotel in Vienna. Not cosy, anyway.

Britten, true to form, died more decorously at home, aged sixty-three, in the arms of Peter Pears, though dying in someone's arms can seldom be comfortable for either party so that one is never sure this isn't simply a figure of speech. For all the sacred music Britten had written, it was Auden who was the believer – both of them, though, ending up commemorated in Westminster Abbey.

Auden It cannot be said too often: what matters is the work.

ASM distributes some new pages. The music is switched off.

Fitz What's this?

Kay You know what it is. We did it yesterday. It's the new ending.

Fitz I still don't see what's wrong with what we've got. It's a nice dying fall. It's in the poet's own words. What's the matter with it?

Author It was something Auden himself said – which is in the play, or was, till you cut it out – how he felt that the end of *The Tempest* really won't do, that it's all very neat but that there's more to be said. And so he lets Caliban speak. That's why the play is called *Caliban's Day*. Look, Auden and Britten are dead, Carpenter died in 2005, the only survivor the boy – which is Caliban again. What happens to him?

Fitz Does it matter? The audience aren't going to care. The punters.

Author Exactly. So it does matter. They have to be made to care. You have to dispose of the boy. They're dead, but Caliban is still with us.

Henry Caliban is always with us.

Kay Let's run it, anyway.

Henry Is he supposed to win, the boy? Because that's sentimental. Those boys don't win.

Tim Your friend at RADA did.

Donald And he lives on. That's winning in anybody's book.

Author Can we just do it?

Kay Yes. Just top and tail it with the other. Fitz.

Auden It cannot be said too often: what matters is the work. That night in Vienna I read from my poem on the death of Yeats.

He recites this faultlessly.

Earth, receive an honoured guest;
William Yeats is laid to rest:
Let the Irish vessel lie
Emptied of its poetry.

Time that is intolerant
Of the brave and innocent,
And indifferent in a week
To a beautiful physique,

Worships language and forgives
Everyone by whom it lives;
Pardons cowardice, conceit,
Lays its honours at their feet.

Time that with this strange excuse
Pardoned Kipling and his views,
And will pardon Paul Claudel,
Pardons him for writing well.

Follow, poet, follow right
To the bottom of the night,
With your unconstraining voice
Still persuade us to rejoice;

In the deserts of the heart
Let the healing fountain start,
In the prison of his days
Teach the free man how to praise.

82

Fitz And that's where I believe it ought to end, with the poetry. *Nobilmente*. Well, it trumps everything else. I'm sorry, love, but I do. And not for me. I don't want the last word. I'm thinking of Auden. That's where the audience will want it to end, anyway.

Author With the boy left out of the account it's too easy. If Auden thought *The Tempest* was too tidy, what is that?

Fitz Let the poet speak, that's all I'm saying.

Kay For the moment I think we should rehearse what is written.

Author Thank you.

Kay Tim.

Stuart Auden asked me that night what it was that I wanted. I didn't know then and I don't altogether know now, but if I had spoken then, this is what I should have said.

Carpenter And the boy stands up like a wild fig tree from monumental marble.

Fitz You see, what does that mean?

Author It's a quotation from Coleridge.

Fitz Who's going to know that?

Tim Are we going to do the scene or not?

Kay Yes, we are. Fitz, behave.

Tim Then he summons Britten back, right? (*Then as Stuart.*) He should come back, for a start.

Britten I have already. I do not need a summons. My famous car has disappeared.

Fitz Is it me? (*Then as Auden.*) So once more Caliban prepares to address the audience.

Tim Am I taking my clothes off?

Fitz Oh, for fuck's sake, does he have to? Nobody'll look at anything else.

Author He has to take his clothes off.

Fitz It's so old-fashioned.

Henry That's not for you to say, is it? He has to take his clothes off because he's saying, 'This is all I have.'

Kay Could we leave it for today and just concentrate on the text? (*Giving cue.*) 'So once more . . .'

Auden So once more Caliban prepares to address the audience.

Stuart No, not Caliban, whoever he was. And not in the language of Henry James, or any other tosser. No. Me. Us. Here. Now. When do we figure and get to say our say? The great men's lives are neatly parcelled for posterity, but what about us? When do we take our bow? Not in biography. Not even in diaries.

    'A boy came round. Picked up on the hill. Didn't stay.'
    'Your grandfather was sucked off by W. H. Auden.'
    'Benjamin Britten sat naked on the side of my bath.'
    Because if nothing else, we at least contributed. We were in attendance, we boys of art. And though there's the odd photograph, nobody remembers who they're of: uncaptioned or 'with an unidentified friend', unnamed girls, unnameable boys, the flings, the tricks. The fodder of art.

Carpenter So what is it you want? A mention? A footnote?

Stuart I want to figure. He goes on about stuff being cosy, England and that. But it's not England that's cosy. It's art, literature, him, you, the lot of you. Because there's always someone left out. You all have a map. I

don't have a map. I don't even know what I don't know.
I want to get in. I want to join. I want to know.

Auden No. You don't want to know. Nobody wants to
know any more.You want what Caliban always wants:
you want to be knowing. We can't help you.

A piano plays 'Show Me the Way to Go Home'.
Auden and Britten are seated, Carpenter leans across
the table between them. Stuart picks up his bag and
opens the door, turns to look back at them, Britten
turns briefly to him, then away.
Stuart closes the door as the music ends.

Kay Thank you. Well done, darlings. Full company ten
o'clock tomorrow.

Fitz It will be better.

Kay (*hugging Fitz*) I know.

Phone rings. Matt answers it.

Fitz And tomorrow I can smoke.

Henry It is bleak. I thought maybe at the finish I should
take his hand?

Author No . . .

Matt Fitz, your car's outside.

Fitz Thank you.

Tim Will you be all right?

Fitz You see, that's what's wrong with *The Tempest*. The
question Caliban never got the chance to ask:
  'Will you be all right, Prospero?'
  I'll be fine, I'll be fine. What's done is done. What's not
done . . . that's done, too. And now for some real work:
  'How would you describe your favourite instant coffee?

85

Because if you are like me it comes with a hint of the hacienda!' Now that is proper acting. Night.

Exits as company call goodnights after him.

Tim Oh dear.

Henry Don't worry. He'll get away with it. He always has. And if he forgets, he's playing someone who does forget. They'll think it's inspired. Whereas I, who know every plodding word, will be thought to have turned in my usual efficient performance.

Kay And thank goodness.

Henry You've seen it all before.

She kisses him.

Donald I've still not found him, have I?

Tim Who?

Donald Carpenter.

Kay It's getting there, love.

Donald Did the music thing help?

Kay makes an equivocal gesture.

It's hard because to me, you see, Carpenter is the centre of the play. Its heart.

Henry (*to Tim, who is wheeling his bike*) Which way are you going?

Tim The pub.

During all this Henry has been hanging around for Tim. They exit.

Donald I wonder if I ought to have a wig.

Kay Tomorrow, darling.

The Author nearly bumps into Donald, who raises a sheepish hand in farewell.

Author Actors. I never get used to them.

Kay Fitz is frightened, that's what it is. But then everybody's frightened. To act is to be frightened. When I used to do it I was always frightened. Threw up before every performance.

Author I didn't know you acted.

Kay Yes. I loved it.

Author What happened?

Kay Nothing. That was the trouble.

Author You were very good this afternoon.

Kay Actors are like soldiers. The soldiers fear the enemy. The actors fear the audience. Fear of failing. Fear of forgetting, fear of art. Olivier ended up terrified. If you sat in the front row you could see him trembling. And besides all that, there's the fear of this building. I worked once or twice with Ronald Eyre. Difficult man and, like all the best directors, an ex-schoolmaster. Ron knew what fear was . . . he'd worked at the RSC and he was here not long after it opened. The opening was, of course, disastrous. Ron said they should have moved out straight away, gone back to the Old Vic and rented the place out, made the Olivier into a skating rink, the Cottesloe a billiard hall and the Lyttelton boxing. Then after twenty-odd years of ordinary unpretentious entertainment, when it's shabby and run-down and been purged of culture, and all the pretension had long since been beaten out of it, then with no fanfare at all they should sneak back with the occasional play and nobody need be frightened any more. Except of course the actors.

He was wrong, though, Ron. Because what's knocked

the corners off the place, taken the shine off it and made it dingy and unintimidating – are plays. Plays plump, plays paltry, plays preposterous, plays purgatorial, plays radiant, plays rotten – but plays persistent. Plays, plays, plays. The habit of art.

Author What happened to him?

Kay Ron? Oh, you know. He died.

The Author is going.

Author But about the play. I am right, aren't I? There is always somebody left out, one way or another.

Kay Oh yes, darling. Every, every time.

He goes, she collects her things, then turns out the lights as she exits.